Applying the new copyright law: A guide for educators and librarians

Jerome K. Miller

Graduate School of Library Science
University of Illinois

American Library Association

Chicago 1979

Library of Congress Cataloging in Publication Data

Miller, Jerome K
    Applying the new copyright law
    Includes bibliographical references and index.
    1. Copyright—United States. 2. Teachers—United
States—Handbooks, manuals, etc. 3. Librarians—United
States—Handbooks, manuals, etc. I. Title.

KF2995.M54   346'.73'0482   79-4694
ISBN 0-8389-0287-1

Dedicated to my parents
in honor of their
Golden Wedding Anniversary

Contents

Contents

Figures

Introduction

This small book was written to help librarians and teachers understand the new U.S. copyright law and to apply it to their work. In writing this book I have been quite conscious of the hazards of treating a specialized field of the law without the benefit of legal training. Readers should understand the limitations this places on the book. They also should recognize that it cannot replace competent legal advice provided by a member of the bar. Future works on this subject will take into account the case law that will develop.

I also have attempted to take a middle ground in interpreting the disputed areas, such as placing photocopies on reserve, the question of "spontaneity," and videotaping television programs. Some are sure to be displeased with the positions I have taken; some will find them too conservative, while others will find them irresponsibly radical. However they may regard the positions I have taken, I hope readers will understand that I have taken them with the advice and encouragement of competent authorities. Professor Roger D. Billings, Jr., of the Salmon P. Chase College of Law, Northern Kentucky University, reviewed and commented on chapters 2, 4, and 5. Sara Case, then associate director of the American Library Association's Washington office, reviewed chapter 3 on library photocopying. My esteemed colleague D. W. Krummel offered many useful comments on chapter 1 on the historical development of copyright. The publisher obtained the assistance of several additional readers whose names are unknown to me and whose comments provided valuable insights for improving the book. Needless to say, the readers' comments have not always been agreement. In dealing with one controversial point, two eminent experts took issue with the position I had taken; one found it too conservative, and the other found it too liberal. In revising the manuscript I took a middle position, which will not please either reader. However pleased or displeased they may be with the final form of the book, I trust they will understand that their contributions are greatly appreciated.

Four excellent graduate or research assistants, Sheila Core, Joanna Sizmur, Lois McTague, and Mary L. Mallory, made substantial contributions in their various roles as proofreader, verifier, indexer, and literary critic. Their help and friendship are greatly appreciated.

I must also acknowledge my indebtedness to many friends who have contributed to my understanding of copyright. Gerald R. Brong introduced me to the subject. Harold E. Hill, Harold E. Wigren, Ivan R. Bender, and Eugene N. Aleinikoff have all helped improve my understanding of the field. Robert E. deKieffer was most helpful in his roles as friend, teacher, and dissertation advisor; portions of chapter 4 are based on that dissertation. Finally, I must acknowledge the contributions of my family. My sister Mary C. Pepin is a constant ally. My brother David, an attorney specializing in future interests and the Internal Revenue Service Code, has been very helpful in improving my understanding of the workings of the legal system. My parents Walter and Kathleen Miller also have been a constant source of encouragement; this book is dedicated to them as a small token of my appreciation.

A brief history of copyright

Copyright originated in Italy in the early Renaissance, when the governing bodies of the city-states granted patents, or exclusive rights, to authors, inventors, and merchants. The oldest recorded patent was awarded by the Florentine Republic in 1421 to Filippo Brunelleschi. The patent was for an improvement in the design of shallow-draft boats. Brunelleschi, as architect of the Florence cathedral dome, was having difficulty moving boatloads of stone over shallow areas of the Arno River. His patent was incorporated in a new boat, the *Badalone*. The design was unsuccessful (the boat sank), but the institution of patents caught on. They were introduced in Venice a few years later. Between 1469 and 1517, the city issued *privilegii* related to printing. Some were exclusive licenses to print books in a certain foreign language, while others were exclusive licenses for printing by a certain method. On September 1, 1486, Marc Antonio Sabellico received the first known copyright for a specific title. He received an exclusive control over the printing and distribution of his *Decades rerum Venetarum*. In January 1491-92, Petrus Franciscus de Ravenna received a copyright for *Foenix*. The practice soon spread to other parts of Europe. Commonly, printers received short-term monopolies for printing the works

1

of certain authors, or certain titles, or books on certain subjects. The division of intellectual creativity between literary works (copyrights) and inventive works (patents) had not arisen yet. The fifteenth and sixteenth century patents also provided short-term monopolies for new industries and trades, thus supplying a foundation for modern, controlled monopolies in transportation, public utilities, and communications.

Printing spread to England in 1476, and within a few years King Henry VII began granting exclusive patents for printing certain types of books. The practice was continued by Henry VIII. After the Act of Supremacy of 1534, the king was anxious to suppress religious dissent. He used his royal prerogative to impose censorship through licensing. Enforcement proved to be difficult. The censorship problem was solved when Queen Mary Tudor granted a charter to the Stationers' Company on May 4, 1557. The Stationers' Company, a trade association, was to enjoy a monopoly on printing, on condition that they print nothing offensive to the Crown. Royal censors were available to determine the suitability of questionable manuscripts and to punish those who printed inappropriate materials. By acquiescing to the Queen's desire to eliminate books unfavorable to her political or religious views, the printers gained a comfortable monopoly on printing. Their monopoly was assured by a right to seek out and destroy presses that were not operated by members of the Company. The charter required printers to record the titles of their books and pamphlets in the Stationers' register prior to printing. This was apparently intended to facilitate the regulation of the press. In time, it served to extend the printers' monopoly. The custom arose that a printer would not print a book or pamphlet registered by a brother printer. Some titles remained long out of print, but no member was allowed to infringe another printer's "copy right." The custom became so well entrenched that, in time, one printer could sue another for infringement of this "copy right."

The "copy right" was the property of the printer. The authors usually did not receive any consideration for their work. Printers sometimes purchased manuscripts from popular authors, but once the manuscript was acquired, the printer retained perpetual rights to the work.

An early form of copyright protection also flourished in the German-speaking nations. During the sixteenth century, the

Holy Roman emperors granted over 350 "authors' privileges," an early form of copyright. The emperors also granted these privileges to artists and composers. Albrecht Dürer was a major beneficiary of these grants. The Duke of Saxony, the Duke of Bavaria, and the municipal bodies of Frankfurt and Leipzig all granted authors' privileges during that period.

In Great Britain the Stationers' Company charter was renewed a number of times. It finally expired in 1695, during the reign of William and Mary. The printers appealed repeatedly to Parliament for a continuation of the system. Fifteen years passed before Parliament arrived at a solution, the Statute of Queen Anne of 1710. It was a remarkable solution. It substantially revised the British system of copyrights and formed the basis of modern copyright. The statute contained a "grandfather clause" renewing copyright in existing works for a period of twenty-one years. These rights were retained by the printers. All books printed on or after April 10, 1710, received copyright protection for fourteen years, and these rights were vested in the authors. If the author was alive at the end of the fourteen-year period, the protection was automatically extended for another fourteen years. The statute required that all books and pamphlets be registered in the records of the Stationers' Company. It also required the copyright owner to deposit nine copies of the work with the Company for distribution to certain designated libraries. There was also an interesting provision for regulating the price of books. This statute is clearly the turning point in the development of copyright. It standardized the process of obtaining protection. It added, perhaps unintentionally, a bit of democracy to copyright. No longer were political connections or membership in an exclusive society needed to obtain a copyright. The law provided a limited duration to the monopoly, as well as an orderly procedure for remedying infringements.

The Massachusetts Bay Colony passed two copyright laws that predate the Statute of Anne. In May 1672, the General Court for Elections of the Massachusetts Bay Colony issued an interesting order:

In ansr to the petition of John Vsher, the Court judgeth it meete
to order, & be it by this Court ordered & enacted, that no printer
shall print any more coppies then are agreed & pajd for by the ouner
of the sajd coppie or coppies, nor shall he nor any other reprint or

> make sale of any of the same, without the sajd ouners consent, vpon
> the forfeiture and poenalty of treble the whole charges of printing,
> & paper &c., of the whole quantity payd for by the ouner of the
> coppie, to the sajd ouner or his assignes.[1]

The order meets all but one of the modern tests for copyright protection. It identifies the person protected, it contains a consent provision (no copies could be printed or sold without the owner's consent), as well as a formula for calculating damages for infringement. It only lacked a duration statement (definition of a period of time during which no one else could print, reprint, or sell the book). John Usher was a well-to-do, second-generation Boston merchant. He imported, published, and sold fine books and dabbled in local politics. He was chosen by the general court to publish a revised edition of the Massachusetts laws. He feared that his printers, Samuel Green and Marmaduke Johnson, might print extra copies and sell them for their own profit. The order of the general court was nicely designed to forestall the problem.

Usher was not satisfied. A year later he again petitioned the general court for a law protecting his interests in the book. The court passed the following decree:

> John Vsher Having been at the sole Chardge of the Impression of the
> booke of Lawes, and presented the Governour, Magistrates, Secretary,
> as also every Deputy, and the Clark of the deputation with one. The
> Curt Judgeth it meete to order that for at least Seven years, Vnless
> he shall have sold them all before that tjme, there shall be no other
> or further Impressions made by any person hereof in this Jurisdiction,
> under the penalty this court shall see cause to lay on any that shall
> adventure in that Kind, besides making ffull sattisfaction to the said
> Jno Vsher or his Assigns, for his chardge and damage thereon. Voted
> by the whole court met together.[2]

Like the law of the previous year, this law identifies the person receiving the protection, it contains a consent provision, and it offers a formula for calculating damages in the event of an infringement. It goes one step further by providing a clearly defined duration of the copyright protection. Unlike the law passed the previous year, it applied only to John Usher. Anyone else wanting copyright protection would have to appeal to the general court for their own protection. Because of this, the second law is more in the nature of an individual patent, much like the ones awarded a century and a half earlier by Kings Henry VII and Henry VIII. The Statute of Anne was the first copyright law to meet all the tests for a true copyright law.

The Statute of Anne applied in the English colonies in North America. The American printers printed few books, but many pamphlets. They were careful not to copy pamphlets published by other American printers. They were famous, though, for reprinting popular pamphlets brought over from London, Edinburgh, and other European cities. The British printers complained, but they did not take legal action to stop the practice.

The American Revolution terminated British copyright in America. There were no copyright laws in America during the war years. Connecticut passed the first American copyright law in January 1783. Massachusetts and Maryland passed similar legislation in March and April of that year. In May the Continental Congress passed a resolution presented by Ralph Izard, James Madison, and Hugh Williamson urging the states to pass copyright laws. It suggested certain features they hoped to see included in the state laws. Twelve states eventually passed copyright laws, Delaware being the exception. Each state's law was a bit different from the others. They were all based on British copyright law, and some borrowed heavily from the laws of other states. Most of the laws protected books and pamphlets. The South Carolina law protected only books, while New York's law also protected papers. The Connecticut, Georgia, and North Carolina laws also protected maps and charts. The variations in state laws and the problems in interstate litigation made them all difficult to enforce. The problem was solved when the responsibility for copyright legislation was given to the federal government. The copyright enabling clause in the Constitution was introduced by Charles C. Pinckney. It reads:

> The Congress shall have power . . . To promote the progress of science and useful arts, by securing, for limited times, to authors and inventors, the exclusive right to their respective writings and discoveries.[3]

The first U.S. copyright statute was passed on May 31, 1790, during the second session of Congress. It was based on the Statute of Anne, with some parts drawn from the state laws. It was amended in 1802 to extend protection to prints and to require a proper copyright notice in each work.

The U.S. copyright laws have undergone four general revisions, in 1831, 1870, 1909, and 1976. The Statute of Anne and the first U.S. law provided a duration of fourteen years, renewable for fourteen more years. The 1831 revision changed this to twenty-eight years, plus fourteen years. Copyright protection was extended to musical compositions and the deposit requirements were changed. The first law required that a copy of each work be deposited in the office of the appropriate U.S. District Court. The 1831 law retained this requirement and further required the clerk of the court to forward a list of the registrations and the depository copies to the Secretary of State. The depository regulations were changed again in 1846, in the law establishing the Smithsonian Institution. Depository copies now were to be sent to the Secretary of State, the Smithsonian Institution Library, and the Library of Congress. The record-keeping and deposit laws were changed again in 1859, when they were moved from the Secretary of State's office to the relatively new Department of the Interior.

In 1856, copyright protection was extended to public performances of dramatic works. The owner of the copyright had the sole right to perform his or her works. Others who wished to perform the works had to obtain the consent of the owner. Permission was usually given in return for a licensing fee. The law was amended again in 1865 to extend protection to photographs.

The second complete revision of the law passed in 1870. Coverage was extended to statuary, models, designs, translations, and dramatizations of copyrighted works. Predictably, the registration and deposit rules were changed again. This time, the entire function was given to the Library of Congress, where it remains today. The depository collections at the Department of the Interior and the Smithsonian Institution were transferred to the Library of Congress.

The 1891 amendment, the so-called International Copyright Act, marked a major change in American copyright and, as a result, in the American publishing industry as well.

The colonial printers had begun the practice of reprinting popular foreign publications without permission. Some early state copyright laws encouraged the practice by limiting protection to local residents. The first U.S. copyright law incorporated this:

... nothing in this act shall be construed to extend to prohibit the importation or vending, reprinting, or publishing within the United States, of any map, chart, book or books, written, printed, or published by any person not a citizen of the United States. ...[4]

The American printers used this loophole to good advantage, soon gaining an international reputation as unprincipled plagiarists. The American intellectual community recognized the evils of this practice and urged a revision of the law. Henry Clay introduced a bill in 1837 permitting foreigners to apply for U.S. copyrights. Since this would be injurious to the publishing industry, his bill included a "manufacturing clause," requiring all copyrighted English language books to be printed in the United States. Literary figures, such as Oliver Wendell Holmes, John Greenleaf Whittier, and Samuel Clemens urged a change in the law. Their urgings were largely overlooked until the international copyright movement reached its climax in the 1880s. The Berne Convention was signed in 1886, but the United States could not participate because it denied copyright protection to foreigners. International copyright legislation was debated in Congress from 1885 until the Chance Bill of 1886 was passed, with revisions, in 1891. The new law included a "manufacturing clause" prohibiting the importation of books published in the English language. An exemption permitted importing as many as two copies of an English language book, as long as they were not intended for resale and they did not include material protected by U.S. copyright. There was no limit on the importation of newspapers, magazines, and foreign language books. The law also permitted the President to "proclaim" that a nation's copyright laws were in harmony with those of the United States or that it was a party to an international copyright agreement acceptable to the United States. This became the legal basis of participation in bilateral copyright agreements. President Harrison immediately "proclaimed" Belgium, France, Great Britain, and Switzerland. Germany, Italy, Denmark, Portugal, Spain, Chile, Mexico, Costa Rica, the Netherlands, Cuba, Norway, and Austria were soon added to the list of "proclaimed" nations. This amendment enabled the United States to join the Mexico City Convention of 1902 and the Buenos Aires Convention of 1910.

The third general revision passed in 1909. It extended the duration of copyright to twenty-eight years, renewable for an additional twenty-eight years. It introduced compulsory licenses for mechanical reproductions of musical works. The producers of recordings were required to pay a royalty fee of "two cents per part" for the recordings they produced. The American Society of Composers, Authors, and Publishers (ASCAP) was established to handle the collection and distribution of the fees. The law was amended in 1912 to extend copyright protection to motion pictures.

It was amended again in 1954 to permit the United States to ratify the Universal Copyright Convention of 1952. This required relaxing or removing the requirements for mechanical reproduction rights in music, certain deposit requirements, and the requirements of the manufacturing clause. The changes in the manufacturing clause permitted the importation of up to 1,500 copies of an English language book within the first five years of its publication. The United States ratified the Universal Copyright Convention in 1954; it took force in 1955.

With the passage of this legislation, the Copyright Office began studying an overall revision of the 1909 copyright law. A special appropriation permitted the Copyright Office to employ experts to prepare reports on difficult aspects of copyright revision. Thirty-five studies were published between 1960 and 1963 under a collective title: *The Copyright Law Revision Studies.* In 1961, the Copyright Office presented "A Report of the Register of Copyrights on the General Revision of the U.S. Copyright Law." Between 1961 and 1964 there were many meetings between the copyright office staff and interested parties, attempting to develop a consensus about the revision bill. A revision bill was introduced in both Houses of Congress in 1964, but Congress did not conduct hearings on it. The Copyright Office responded to criticisms of the bill by issuing a revised bill that was introduced in both Houses on February 4, 1965. Hearings were conducted during the next eleven years. The much revised bill was finally passed and signed by President Ford on October 19, 1976. Most parts of the bill went into effect January 1, 1978.

The Copyright Law of 1976 marks several important departures from old copyright law. Rights fall into two groups, owner's rights and user's rights. The copyright owner's rights have been extended in a number of ways. The jukebox exemption was terminated; jukebox owners must now pay an eight-dollar per machine per year license. The cable television (CATV) exemption was also closed. Almost all CATV operators must now pay a royalty for the transmission of distant stations; the fees are based on their gross receipts and the types of programs they carry. The exemption for nonprofit radio and television stations was also terminated; they must pay royalties for the musical, literary, and pictorial works they use. The duration of copyright protection was extended to the life of the author plus fifty years, in keeping with the practices found in most industrial nations. Anonymous works and works made for hire are protected for seventy-five years. Foreign authors and publishers will benefit from the gradual phaseout of the manufacturing clause.

The new law also institutes a number of guarantees for the user of the copyrighted materials. The judicial interpretation of fair use now has statutory force. This includes special dispensations for photocopying and other forms of duplication by schools, libraries, and archives. Special exemptions are provided for the blind and the deaf.

The protracted study of the revision bill and a pressing need for change prompted Congress to remove two sections of the bill and pass them separately. Based on the decision in *White-Smith* v. *Apollo* (1908), copyright protection was never available for sound recordings. The rapid growth of tape piracy in the 1960s required a prompt change in the law. Congress passed the Sound Recording Amendment of 1971, based on a section of the copyright revision bill then before Congress. It extended copyright protection to sound recordings. Another important section establishing the National Commission on the New Technological Uses of Copyrighted Works (CONTU) was separated from the rest of the bill and passed in December 1974. This commission is responsible for examining problems in the use of copyrighted materials in computers and developing recommendations for legislation in the computer area and other problem areas.

Copyright revision has not stopped with the passage of the 1976 Copyright Revision Act. The Copyright Office is studying the possibility of recommending legislation extending copyright protection to typefaces. The Copyright Office, with the encouragement of certain members of Congress, is considering an amendment that would give performers a portion of the royalties earned from the sale and performance of the copyrighted work. CONTU will soon recommend an amendment regulating the use of copyrighted works in computers. The Copyright Office is required to conduct periodic studies on certain aspects of the law and to recommend needed amendments to Congress. Finally, the new law will certainly be altered by judicial decisions. Copyright has evolved over the past five centuries; it will continue to change in the future.

Fair use  2

Fair use is, without question, one of the most difficult and contrary concepts in the corpus of copyright law. It is, in fact, a contradiction of the fundamental copyright concept. From its inception, copyright has been a vehicle for granting an author, or his or her heirs, an exclusive monopoly in the author's creative works. Fair use contradicts this by conferring certain rights on persons other than the author or heirs. Moreover, this right may be exercised without paying a fee or informing the copyright owner. It is not surprising that it is controversial.

Fair use originated as a court-made doctrine long before it appeared in statutes. In 1802 Lord Ellenborough, a British jurist, spoke of a work being "used fairly." In 1810 Lord Eldon spoke of a "legitimate use" and "fair quotations." The term *fair use* first appeared in a British case in 1869.[1] Fair use was incorporated in U.S. common law in the nineteenth century. A fair use provision was considered for inclusion in the U.S. Copyright Revision Act of 1909, but Congress decided that the matter should be left to the courts. Several copyright revision bills that included fair use provisions were introduced during the 1920s and 1930s. The question was revived in 1955 when the Copyright Office began the research that led to the Copyright Revision Act of 1976. Many eminent legal scholars and copyright attorneys urged Congress not to legislate the question, but to let the courts continue to handle it. Publishers, media producers, educators, and librarians insisted on a statutory provision to clarify the issue. Their wish was heard and a fair use section was included in the law.

The fair use issue was divided into two parts: Section 108, "Limitations on Exclusive Rights: Reproduction by Libraries and Archives," and Section 107, "Limitations on Exclusive Rights: Fair Use." Unfortunately, Section 108 has a distinctively library-oriented title, while Section 107 is simply titled "Fair Use." This led many readers to view them as isolated and unrelated elements. They are, in fact, interrelated parts of the larger fair use issue.

Definitions

Many scholars have attempted to define fair use, and none has quite succeeded. Ball defined it as

> [a] privilege in others than the owner of the copyright to use the copyrighted material in a reasonable manner without his consent, notwithstanding the monopoly granted to the owner of the copyright.[2]

The Copyright Act describes fair use as a use

> of a copyrighted work, including such use by reproduction ... for purposes such as criticism, comment, news reporting, teaching (including multiple copies for classroom use), scholarship, or research. ...[3]

The Senate report calls it an "equitable rule of reason," which by its nature defies definition.[4]

The criteria

Most scholars and lawmakers find it impossible to write an acceptable definition of fair use. They prefer a set of criteria that can be used to determine individual cases. The literature offers many sets of fair use criteria. The authors of the new law drew on the common law to provide four criteria for determining individual cases:

1. the purpose and character of the use, including whether such use is of a commercial nature or is for nonprofit educational purposes;
2. the nature of the copyrighted work;
3. the amount and substantiality of the portion used in relation to the copyrighted work as a whole; and
4. the effect of the use upon the potential market for or value of the copyrighted work.[5]

They are not easy to understand. Fortunately, new laws are accompanied by committee reports that provide a commentary on the law. The new copyright law is accompanied by three important reports: House report No. 94-1476, Senate report No. 94-473, and the Conference Committee report, issued as House report No. 94-1733. With the aid of these reports, the four criteria can be explained in more precise terms. These reports will probably carry considerable weight in future court cases as evidence of the "intent of the legislators." Although they are quite important, they are not the law, and the courts are free to ignore them.

Purpose and character

Purpose and character are clarified in the Senate report.

Nonprofit use. Fair use is not restricted to nonprofit institutions, but greater latitude is given for nonprofit uses. Two points must be considered: (1) Will the copies be used in a nonprofit institution? and (2) Will there be a charge for the copies? A teacher in a commercial school who charges students for copies of copyrighted works probably has no basis for claiming that the copying was a fair use. A teacher in a nonprofit school who makes multiple copies of a copyrighted work and distributes them to the pupils without charge has a better claim that this is a fair use.

Spontaneity. The Senate report is quite clear on this point:

> The fair use doctrine in the case of classroom copying would apply primarily to the situation of a teacher who, acting individually and at his own volition, makes one or more copies for temporary use by himself or his pupils in the classroom. A different result is indicated where the copying was done by the educational institution, school system, or larger unit or where copying was required or suggested by the school administration, either in special instances or as part of a general plan.[6]

A second aspect of spontaneity is found in section 107 of the House report, "Agreement on Guidelines for Classroom Copying in Not-for-Profit Educational Institutions" (hereafter referred to in the text as the Agreement on Guidelines):

> The inspiration and decision to use the work and the moment of its use for maximum teaching effectiveness are so close in time that it would be unreasonable to expect a timely reply to a request for permission.[7]

It is important to differentiate between these two aspects of spontaneity. The first element (that the teacher must make or request copies at his or her own volition) is an imperative. It must not be overlooked. The second element (copying when time does not permit seeking permission) is an added element found in the Agreement on Guidelines. Contrary to a common misunderstanding, it is *not* a *limiting* factor to deprive teachers and others of their right to make single or multiple copies of copyrighted works when time *does* permit seeking permission. This second spontaneity factor (no time to seek permission) is an *added* factor to give teachers greater latitude in meeting unforeseen problems and opportunities in the classroom. Nearly every teacher has experienced moments when a well-planned lesson failed because of an unforeseen problem. Distributing copies of an essay or article may be the necessary element to get the lesson back on course. Resourceful teachers also use current events as examples or focal points for effective lessons. These problems and opportunities usually occur with little warning. If there is not enough time to seek permission to make the copies, teachers may assume a bit more latitude in fair use copying to meet this need.

The second spontaneity factor should not be interpreted to forbid fair use copying when there is ample time to seek permission. It is also not intended to be a crutch for teachers who do their lesson planning at the last moment. It only stresses the idea that greater latitude applies to spur-of-the-moment copying to fit the "teachable moment." This obviously raises the question about the time required to receive a "timely reply." The law and the reports do not offer guidance on this point, but the Association of American Publishers recommends allowing four weeks for a publisher to receive a request, act on it, and respond.[8] That is probably the best answer for the present. It should be added that writing for permission is only expected for making multiple copies of articles, essays, and other parts of books.

Single and multiple copying. There is a general agreement that teachers may make single copies of articles, essays, poems, illustrations, chapters of books, and the like for the purpose of research, study, and lesson planning. Congress was more concerned about the practice of making multiple copies of copyrighted works for class distribution. In its final form, the law clearly gives teachers the right to make multiple copies of copyrighted works for class distribution, but the amount of copying must be limited. The Senate report identifies three limitations: (1) Only enough copies may be made to distribute to the class; (2) copies may not be distributed outside the class; (3) it suggests that the copies be recalled and destroyed after the use.[9] Inasmuch as most pupils discard school "handouts" at the end of the semester, or earlier, this may satisfy the third point. The Agreement on Guidelines offers specific *minimum* recommendations for multiple copying:

II. Multiple Copies for Classroom Use

Multiple copies (not to exceed in any event more than one copy per pupil in a course) may be made by or for the teacher giving the course for classroom use or discussion; *provided that:*

A. The copying meets the tests of brevity and spontaneity as defined below; *and,*

B. Meets the cumulative effect test as defined below; *and,*

C. Each copy includes a notice of copyright.

Definitions

Brevity

(i) Poetry: (a) A complete poem if less than 250 words and if printed on not more than two pages or, (b) from a longer poem, an excerpt of not more than 250 words.

(ii) Prose: (a) Either a complete article, story or essay of less than 2,500 words, or (b) an excerpt from any prose work of not more than 1,000 words or 10% of the work, whichever is less, but in any event a minimum of 500 words.

[Each of the numerical limits stated in "i" and "ii" above may be expanded to permit the completion of an unfinished line of a poem or of an unfinished prose paragraph.]

(iii) Illustration: One chart, graph, diagram, drawing, cartoon or picture per book or per periodical issue.

(iv) "Special" works: Certain works in poetry, prose or in "poetic prose" which often combine language with illustrations and

15

which are intended sometimes for children and at other times for a more general audience fall short of 2,500 words in their entirety. Paragraph "ii" above notwithstanding such "special works" may not be reproduced in their entirety; however, an excerpt comprising not more than two of the published pages of such special work and containing not more than 10% of the words found in the text thereof, may be reproduced.

Spontaneity
(This section was discussed earlier on page 13.)

Cumulative Effect
(i) The copying of the material is for only one course in the school in which the copies are made.
(ii) Not more than one short poem, article, story, essay or two excerpts may be copied from the same author, nor more than three from the same collective work or periodical volume during one class term.
(iii) There shall not be more than nine instances of such multiple copying for one course during one class term.
   [The limitations stated in "ii" and "iii" above shall not apply to current news periodicals and newspapers and current news sections of other periodicals.][10]
(The complete text is reproduced in Appendix A.)

These are *minimum* guidelines developed by the Ad Hoc Committee on Copyright Law Revision, the Authors League of America, and the Association of American Publishers. The opening sentence of the agreement states: "The purpose of the following guidelines is to state the minimum and not the maximum standards of educational fair use...."[11] Educators who limit multiple copying to these guidelines may rest assured that they will not be sued for copyright infringements. Harold E. Wigren, one of the authors of the guidelines, stresses that they should NOT be regarded as the outer limits of legal copying.[12] Copying in excess of these guidelines may well be a fair use of the copyrighted materials.

The two great problems in applying these minimum guidelines center on (1) the limit of nine instances of copying per class per term, and (2) the 2,500-word limitation. Nine instances of copying per class per term is probably quite adequate for most classes, but it places a heavy burden on teachers offering current awareness or reading courses. Again, this number is an arbitrary figure designed to interpret a vague and flexible section of the law. It is also, as the authors state, a minimum number. Copying in excess of that number can readily fall within the bounds of fair use. The 2,500-word limitation may be appropriate for copying from children's books, but it is an unreasonable limitation for college-level teaching. Scholarly articles, which are the staple of college-level required reading, run to multiples of 2,500 words. This point in the guidelines, as it applies to most required readings, contradicts both the spirit of the fair use section and other points of the guidelines (for example, one article or one essay). Interpreted literally, it changes the guidelines to read "four to six pages of a scholarly article" or "four to six pages of an essay." This point can safely be ignored when applying the guidelines to copying periodical articles and essays for class distribution. It is unfortunate that we must puzzle over these points in attempting to apply the fair use criteria. Court decisions will eventually supply clearer answers. In the meantime, good judgment will solve most problems. When questions arise about the legality of copying a work, the publisher's permission to make the copies should be obtained. (Writing for permission is treated in chapter 4.)

Collections and anthologies. Publishers and media producers willingly accept isolated copying by teachers. Their major concern, however, is that repeated copying will lead to the development of collections or anthologies that will deprive them of legitimate sales. The Senate report recognized this problem:

> Spontaneous copying of an isolated extract by a teacher, which may be a fair use under appropriate circumstances, could turn into an infringement if the copies were accumulated over a period of time with other parts of the same work, or were collected with other materials from various works so as to constitute an anthology.[13]

The Agreement on Guidelines states:

> Copying shall not be used to create or to replace or substitute for anthologies, compilations or collective works. Such replacement or substitution may occur whether copies of various works or excerpts therefrom are accumulated or reproduced and used separately.[14]

Student copying. The Senate report provides for "special uses" by students as a part of the learning process.

> There are certain classroom uses which, because of their special nature, would not be considered an infringement in the ordinary

case. For example, copying of extracts by pupils as exercises in a
shorthand or typing class or for foreign language study. . . .

Likewise, a single reproduction of excerpts from a copyrighted
work by a student calligrapher . . . in a learning situation would be
a fair use of the copyrighted work.[15]

Under these circumstances, almost any copying done by students as a part of the learning process could probably be regarded as a fair use of the copyrighted material. This would seem to include work by student photographers, student audio or video technicians, student printers, and so on. The situation should be reexamined, though, if the copies are commercially exploited, or become part of the school's teaching materials collection, or are produced in excess of a minimum number of copies. (It would be very difficult for a student to master the operation of an offset press by printing only single copies.) The copies probably should be erased or destroyed after they have served their purpose.

Nature of the copyrighted work

The amount of copying performed within the limits of fair use is greatly affected by the nature of the material being copied. A teacher may freely copy news articles from a newspaper, but he or she is strictly enjoined from copying a standard examination. Five types of works are identified for special consideration.

News. The Senate report comments:

With respect to material in newspapers and periodicals the doctrine
of fair use should be liberally applied to allow copying of items of
current interest to supplement and update the students' textbooks,
but this would not extend to copying from periodicals published
primarily for student use.[16]

Periodicals published primarily for student use are usually sold in bulk quantities for class use. They are given special protection, since copying from them often reduces their sales.

Commercially published newsletters, such as *CableLibraries* or *The Kiplinger Newsletter,* are also singled out for special protection. The Senate report explains:

It is argued that newsletters are particularly vulnerable to mass
photocopying, and that most newsletters have fairly modest

circulations. Whether the copying of portions of a newsletter is an act of infringement or a fair use must be judged by the general provisions of this legislation. However, the copying of even a short portion of a newsletter may have a significant impact on the commercial market for the work.[17]

This provision applies to independent newsletters, not to house organs and publicity newsletters.

School publications. The Senate report comments:

Text books and other material prepared primarily for the school markets would be less susceptible to reproduction for classroom use than material prepared for general public distribution.[18]

Consumable materials. The Senate report states plainly, "[W]here the copyright[ed] work is intended to be 'consumable' in the course of classroom activities . . . the privilege of fair use by teachers or pupils would have little if any application."[19] Consumable materials include standard tests, workbooks, answer sheets, and exercise sheets. Copying this material is a copyright infringement on two counts. It violates the "single use" function of the material, and it runs afoul of the fourth fair use criterion, "the effect of the use on the potential market for or value of the work." (More on this later.) In addition to being a copyright infringement, reproducing consumable materials can be a violation of a contractual agreement. Much of this material is sold under a contractual agreement (the fine print in the catalog and on the invoice) that specifically forbids duplicating the material. The Agreement on Guidelines adds:

There shall be no copying of or from works intended to be "consumable" in the course of study or of teaching. These include workbooks, exercises, standardized tests and test booklets and answer sheets and like consumable material.[20]

Performance materials. Performance materials include music, drama, motion pictures, filmstrips, and any other materials intended for public performance. Because of the complexity of this subject, it is treated in a separate section of this chapter. (See pages 34-57.)

"Implied consent" to duplicate. Implied consent is not mentioned in the copyright law or in the accompanying reports. Implied consent is a theory that suggests that fair use derives

from the author's implied or tacit consent to a small amount of copying from the work for the benefit of society. DeWolf offers some support for the theory.[21] Cohen seems to be of two minds about it:

> "Implied consent" is really no more than a convenient fiction by which the courts reached conclusions prompted by the policies discussed . . . above.
>
> There are circumstances, however, when talk of implied consent does make sense.[22]

Nimmer says implied consent is "manifestly a fiction. . . ."[23] It is outside the scope of this work to resolve this theoretical problem. It does seem desirable to supply a new and narrower interpretation to this convenient phrase—any work that is sold or otherwise distributed for the obvious purpose of being duplicated, and which does not forbid copying or stipulate a duplication or license fee, includes the copyright owner's "implied consent" to duplicate the work in the intended manner and for the intended purpose. A number of firms serving the school market offer publications that are obviously intended to be duplicated in quantity for classroom use. They fall into three groups: (1) certain parts of teacher's manuals, (2) preprinted mimeograph masters, and (3) transparency masters. Teacher's manuals are usually written by the authors of textbooks to supply additional information and materials to help teachers make the best use of the textbook. These manuals identify the goals and objectives for each chapter of the book and make suggestions for teaching each chapter. Some of them provide sample work sheets, exercises, and examinations coordinated to each chapter. They may also include transparency masters coordinated to key points in the book. Textbook publishers donate them to teachers who are using the textbook. Sample copies are also sent to schools that have expressed interest in adopting the textbook.

The second group, preprinted ditto or mimeograph masters, contain student work sheets, examinations, and the like. Some are coordinated with specific textbooks, while others may be used with many textbooks. The nature of mimeograph and ditto machines limits the number of legible copies that can be produced from one master.

The third group, transparency masters, are sold at a nominal cost or distributed free of charge by the manufacturers of overhead projectors and overhead projector film. It is a reasonable assumption that the availability of these masters stimulates the sale of transparency film.

The new law does not seem to touch on the duplication of these materials. As a consequence, teachers are asking if the limit on multiple copying also applies to these materials. The very nature of the materials indicates that they were designed and distributed to be duplicated. The mimeograph and transparency masters are nearly worthless until they are copied.

A sensible "rule of reason" suggests that any work sold or otherwise distributed for the obvious purpose of being duplicated that does not specifically forbid copying or stipulate a duplication license fee includes the copyright owner's "implied consent" to duplicate it in the intended manner and for the intended purpose. Educators who act within these limits in copying these materials should not include this copying in the limits on multiple copying.

Educators should not confuse the above "implied consent" materials with material sold for the purpose of being duplicated that requires a license for copying. An obvious example is "cleared music." These recordings provide numerous short segments of music designed to be included as background music in audiovisual programs. The producers of these materials offer a variety of licensing arrangements for the duplications of the musical segments. Many firms also offer sound effects records under similar licensing arrangements. (See "Cleared Music," pages 99-102.)

Amount and substantiality of the portion used

Amount. The difficult question is how much of a work a teacher may copy under the terms of fair use. Congress did not provide easy formulas to establish the amount. The clearest explanation appears in the Senate report:

> During the consideration of this legislation there has been considerable discussion of the difference between an "entire work" and an "excerpt." The educators have sought a limited right for a teacher to make a single copy of an "entire" work for classroom purposes, but it seems apparent that this was not generally intended to extend beyond a "separately cognizable" or "self-contained" portion (for example, a single poem, story, or article) in a collective work, and that no privilege is sought to reproduce an entire collective work (for example,

an encyclopedia volume, a periodical issue) or a sizeable integrated work published as an entity (a novel, treatise, monograph, and so forth). With this limitation, and subject to the other relevant criteria, the requested privilege of making a single copy appears appropriately to be within the scope of fair use.

The educators also sought statutory authority for the privilege of making "a reasonable number of copies or phonorecords for excerpts or quotations***, provided such excerpts or quotations are not substantial in length in proportion to their source." In general, and assuming the other necessary factors are present, the copying for classroom purposes of extracts or portions, which are not self-contained and which are relatively "not substantial in length" when compared to the larger, self-contained work from which they are taken, should be considered fair use. Depending on the circumstances, the same would also be true of very short self-contained works such as a brief poem, a map in a newspaper, a "vocabulary builder" from a monthly magazine, and so forth. This should not be construed as permitting a teacher to make multiple copies of the same work on a repetitive basis or for continued use.[24]

This has been interpreted in the Agreement on Guidelines:

I. Single Copying for Teachers
A single copy may be made of any of the following by or for a teacher at his or her individual request for his or her scholarly research or use in teaching or preparation to teach a class:
A. A chapter from a book;
B. An article from a periodical or newspaper;
C. A short story, short essay or short poem, whether or not from a collective work;
D. A chart, graph, diagram, drawing, cartoon or picture from a book, periodical, or newspaper.[25]
(The section on making multiple copies for classroom use is reproduced on page 15 of this chapter. The entire document appears in Appendix A.)

Availability. The question of the amount and substantiality of the portion that may be copied must be considered in relation to the availability of the work.

Unpublished works (e.g., manuscripts, letters, notes, diaries) may not be available outside an archive. In spite of this inconvenience, one may not copy these materials without the permission of the author or his or her heirs. The author's "right of first publication" takes priority over all other considerations. The owner of the copy is frequently unable to give permission to make copies. This is especially true in the case of correspondence. The recipient of the correspondence may sell or display the letter, but the "right of first publication" (or the right to make copies) rests with the author or with his or her heirs.

Published materials that are out of print are not as rigidly protected. If an educator makes a diligent search for a copy of an out-of-print work and cannot find an unused copy at a "reasonable price," he or she may have sufficient justification to make single copy or multiple copies of part of it for educational purposes. (See page 132 for a discussion of "reasonable price.") Many out-of-print books and journals are available from reprint and microform publishers. (For a library's right to duplicate out-of-print works, see pages 77-79.) If the work is available from one of these firms, then it cannot be regarded as unavailable. The fact that it is not available in the desired format (i.e., in print, as opposed to microform format) would not justify copying a large part of the work. The Agreement on Guidelines (House report, section 107) probably does not support duplicating an out-of-print work in its entirety. This privilege is available only to libraries and archives through section 108(e). (See pages 77-79.)

Effect on the potential market

The effect of copying on the potential market of a work is, without doubt, the easiest criterion to apply. It is also the most important criterion. If copying all or part of a work *tends* to reduce the volume of the publisher's or producer's sales, then it is certainly an infringement. In addition, if a number of isolated acts taken in aggregate *tend* to reduce the sales of a work, it is an infringement. Effect on potential market is undoubtedly the most important criterion; it must be applied with great care.

Applying the criteria

All four criteria—purpose and character, nature of the work, amount and substantiality of the portion used, and effect on potential market—must be considered in each application of fair use. It is not sufficient to satisfy one criterion and then to assume that the rest do not apply. The fair use checklist may be useful in applying the criteria and their subsections. You may wish to photocopy the list and keep it on your desk or beside the copying machine to help you remember the four criteria and their subsections.

Examples: Making paper copies of printed materials

The following examples are provided to help readers apply the fair use criteria to everyday situations. Please use the fair use checklist in attempting to solve the problems. It may be more convenient to photocopy the checklist so it can be placed alongside the example and answer.

Example 1: A teacher in a public school is preparing a unit on the history of the state. She finds a relevant five-page article in a magazine and photocopies it for use in her work. When she is finished with the copy, it is filed for future use. *Answer:* Part IA does not present a problem. Part IB1 is not a problem, but a question is raised about IB2. The copy is not needed immediately, so she has time to write for permission. Whether spontaneous or planned, it is not necessary to write for permission to make a single photocopy of an article. It is only necessary to write for permission to make multiple copies of articles *in excess* of the guidelines or to copy a *substantial part* of a magazine. Part ID raises a question. The copy will be retained in a file with other articles, clippings, and pamphlets on the same general topic. This is a technical infringement. Most writers take a liberal view on this point; as long as it is a private research file and it does not substitute for purchasing an anthology, it is a fair use.

The second criterion does not present a problem, since magazine articles are not among the closely protected materials identified in this section. The third criterion does not present a problem, since this photocopying falls within the guidelines in IIIB. The fourth criterion does not present a problem unless the publisher sells offprints (copies) of the articles as a profit-making venture.

Example 2: The teacher in Example 1 places the photocopy on the resource shelf in her classroom. The resource shelf contains boxes of pamphlets, photocopies, clippings, paperbacks, and entire issues of magazines. Students who are writing papers and preparing oral reports consult the files for information. File materials are also used for supplemental or

This is a review device to help readers apply the fair use criteria. It cannot substitute for a careful study of the criteria.

I. The purpose and character of the use
    A. The nonprofit character of the use
        1. The copies are used in a nonprofit institution.
        2. No charge is made for the copies.
    B. Spontaneity
        1. The copies are made by or for a teacher or other patron at his or her own volition.
        2. The immediacy of the need does not permit seeking permission to make the copy or copies.
    C. The number of copies made
        1. Single copies of articles, essays, poems, or other small sections of a work are made for private research, study, or class preparation.
        2. Multiple copies for class distribution meet the following requirements:
            a. Only one copy per student.
            b. Copies are not distributed outside the class.
            c. Only a limited number of multiple copies are made each term.
    D. The copy or copies will not be incorporated in a collection or anthology.
    E. Greater latitude applies to copying by students as a learning exercise.

II. The nature of the copyrighted work
    A. Greater latitude applies to copying newspapers and news magazines, except school news magazines and newsletters.
    B. Little copying is permitted from textbooks and other school materials.
    C. Consumable materials may not be copied.
    D. Copying from performance materials is limited.
    E. Certain materials are sold with an "implied consent" to copy.

III. The amount and substantiality of the portion used in relation to the work as a whole
    A. One may copy a chapter from a book.
    B. One may copy an article from a periodical or newspaper.
    C. One may copy an essay or a poem from a collected work.
    D. One may copy an illustration from a book, magazine, or newspaper.
    E. No repetitive multiple copying of the same material is permitted.

IV. The effect of the use on the potential market for or value of the work
    A. If an incident of copying displaces a sale, it is not a fair use.
    B. If several incidents of copying have the cumulative effect of displacing a sale, they are not a fair use.

Fig. 1. A fair use checklist

incentive reading by students who finish their assignments quickly.

Answer: The question can be answered using the fair use checklist. Criteria IA through IC remain the same. The problem centers on ID. The answer is in the Senate report:

Spontaneous copying of an isolated extract by a teacher, which may be a fair use under appropriate circumstances, could turn into an infringement if the copies . . . were collected with other material from various works so as to constitute an anthology.[26]

If the resource shelf contains a number of photocopies on the history of the state, then this is a collection or anthology, which constitutes an infringement. If the resource shelf is a random collection of clippings, pamphlets, whole issues of periodicals, articles torn from magazines, and the like, then the presence of a few photocopies might not be an infringement. The remaining fair use criteria are unchanged from Example 1.

Example 3: Instead of placing a photocopy of the article on the resource shelf, the teacher makes enough photocopies of the article to distribute to the class. She decides on this course of action six weeks before the students begin studying the unit.

Answer: We should first examine criteria IC2 in the checklist. She only makes enough copies to distribute one copy to each student in the class. No additional copies are made, and no copies are distributed outside of the class. The key question is IC2c; does the teacher make photocopies for class distribution frequently or infrequently? The Agreement on Guidelines suggests that a teacher may make multiple copies of copyrighted works for class distribution nine times a term, not counting copies made from newspapers and news magazines. These are acknowledged to be minimum guidelines. If the teacher does not exceed these guidelines, then she is assuredly safe, as long as the other criteria are met. If she greatly exceeds this amount, then she must begin seeking permission to make the copies.

Example 4: A teacher gives a student a short list of appropriate magazine articles on the student's term paper topic and suggests that the student photocopy them so he can work on the assignment at home.

Answer: The teacher did not make the copies or require the student to copy them. The student was free to read and take notes in the library. As long as the student makes the copies on his own volition, the fair use question applies to the student rather than the teacher.

An examination of the checklist does not reveal any limitation on the number of photocopies a student may make in the process of completing assignments. In fact, IE affords students great latitude in this matter. There is little doubt that this is a fair use of the copyrighted materials.

Example 5: A teacher identifies two periodical articles, an encyclopedia article, and a short essay she wants her students to read during the semester. There are eighty students in three sections of the class. Instead of reproducing eighty copies of each article for class distribution, she requests that the school make eight copies of each article (one for every ten students) and that the copies be placed on reserve for assigned reading. The copies are discarded at the end of the semester.

Answer: The answer in Example 3 applies here. As long as the number of articles, essays, and so on, that are chosen for multiple copying does not exceed reasonable limits (the guidelines suggest nine times per class per term) and the other criteria are met, it is a fair use. The fact that she reduces the cost of the operation by making 32 copies (8 copies of four items) instead of 320 copies does not appear to change the issue. The fact that an employee other than the teacher makes the copies also does not change the issue. The decision is made by the teacher, acting on her own volition.

Example 6: A teacher makes multiple copies of a poem for class distribution. In so doing, she meets all the fair use criteria. The lesson is successful, so she decides to make multiple copies of the poem for class distribution in subsequent terms.

Answer: The Senate report is quite explicit on item IIIF in the checklist. A teacher is not permitted "to make multiple copies of the same work on a repetitive basis or for continued use."[27] The teacher needs to obtain the permission of the publisher for the second and subsequent distributions of the poem. If the teacher knows the poem will be used in more than one semester, she should obtain permission before making any copies.

Example 7: The faculty uses an in-service day to study copyright and to write a school policy on some of the controversial issues, such as the number of articles, essays, and poems distributed each semester in multiple copies. During a subsequent semester, a teacher uses her voluntary allotment of uncleared multiple copying for the semester (*uncleared* means copying for which she does not obtain the publisher's permission). For some unforeseen and unpreventable reason, the lesson planned for one afternoon cannot be used. The teacher uses her lunch break to find a short essay and makes enough copies to distribute to the class. The students spend the period reading the article, and devising and acting out alternate conclusions to the article.

Answer: The copyright law limits copying for classroom distribution, but it is not inflexible. Assuming all other criteria were met, IB2 excuses *infrequent,* emergency copying in excess of the limits.

Example 8: Teachers frequently require students to read certain encyclopedia articles. So many articles are cut out of the school's encyclopedias that the teachers are asked to stop assigning specific encyclopedia articles. Some teachers duplicate the key articles for class distribution.

Answer: The answer to Example 3 applies to small amounts of multiple copying from encyclopedias. On the other hand, if the copies are to be made for the purpose of using them in two or more classes or over more than one school term, then permission must be obtained in advance. A "little fair use" hardly applies in this situation. Research indicates that the encyclopedia publishers are very prompt and cooperative in giving teachers permission to duplicate encyclopedia articles for class distribution.[28]

Example 9: A school stretches its investment in work sheets, workbooks, standard tests, and similar single-use materials by duplicating them and having students use the copies.

Answer: This constitutes duplication of consumable materials (IIC) and displacement of a sale (IVA).

Example 10: A school stretches its investment in work sheets and similar consumable materials by laminating them (preserving them by bonding a clear sheet of plastic to each side of the page). Students use grease pencils or washable felt-tip pens to supply the answers, and the marks are subsequently removed with a moist cloth. This permits the school to use the items many times.

Answer: This might slip by IIC on a technicality, because there is no copying. It appears to infringe under IVA because it deprives the publisher of a legitimate sale. (The author takes a conservative position on this point, a position not shared by some authorities, who view it as a fair use since it does not involve copying.)

Example 11: A school stretches its investment in standard tests by requiring students to write their answers on separate answer sheets instead of entering them in the answer spaces on the examination. This permits the school to use the examination sheets several times.

Answer: The answer to Example 10 applies here.

Example 12: A school adopts a new textbook. The textbook is accompanied by a teacher's manual that provides sample work sheets and examinations for each chapter in the textbook. The teacher makes multiple copies of the work sheets and examinations for use in several consecutive semesters.

Answer: Normally a teacher cannot expect to make multiple copies for repeated use under item IIIE or multiple copies of a large part of a copyrighted work under item IIIA-C. In this instance, the publisher provides the teacher's manual to complement and facilitate the use of the textbook. The teacher may be assumed to have the publisher's "implied consent" under item IIE for substantial and repeated copying from the teacher's manual, as long as the copies are used in conjunction with the publisher's textbook. This provision would not apply if the manual contains a statement forbidding the duplication of the materials or requiring a fee for making the copies.

Example 13: A school adopts a new textbook but the teacher prefers to use some of the exercises in the teacher's manual that accompanied the previous textbook. He continues to reproduce multiple copies of the exercise sheets from the old manual for use in several subsequent semesters.

Answer: Having selected a textbook for a course, it is questionable if publishers of competing textbooks give their "implied consent" to substantial and repeated multiple copying from their teacher's manuals. Item IIB greatly limits the amount of materials that may be copied from instructional manuals. One should obtain the publisher's permission for this action.

Example 14: A mathematics teacher makes extensive use of "thought problems" (for example, Mary's parents gave her five dollars for her birthday. She bought a pocketknife for one dollar, a comb for fifteen cents. . . . How much money does she have left?) in his homework assignments and examinations. He writes most of these questions himself, but he also reads math textbooks, curriculum guides, teacher's manuals, and such materials seeking problems to add to his collection.

Answer: This is probably fair use. The fact that the material is reproduced in multiple copies and used in repeated semesters (item IIIE) should be offset by the extraordinarily small amount of copying from any single source and the fact that the copied material represents a small part of the teacher's assignments and examinations.

Example 15: A teacher developed an audio-tutorial program for her biology course. She wrote most of the instructional units, but she duplicated a four- to six-page unit from each of four textbooks. The copies will be distributed to the students in the class. The materials will be used for one semester, and then they will be replaced by teacher-written materials.

Answer: Textbooks and other instructional materials are closely protected from copying in IIB. The amount of material copied from each textbook represents a small part of the book. The amount of copyrighted materials reproduced represents a small part of the materials distributed to the students during the term. This is probably a fair use, if the other criteria are met.

Example 16: A teacher developed an audio-tutorial instructional program. The textual materials distributed to students were almost all copied from textbooks and other instructional materials. The teacher wrote to the publishers seeking permission for the copying. Some publishers required fee payments, which the school agreed to pay. Several publishers refused to give the school permission to make the copies, with or without a fee. If the school wanted to use the materials, the publishers insisted that the school would have to buy one copy of the text for each student in the class.

Answer: It is understandable that some publishers require a copying fee since this sort of thing can reduce the sales of the textbooks. It is unfortunate that there are still some textbook publishers who will not permit the use of their materials in any mode other than the one developed in their textbooks. If the many schools facing this problem were to refuse to adopt these firms' textbooks, it might alter the publishers' behavior. When publishers refuse to permit copying from their books, one may not copy the material. Once permission is denied, the copying cannot be passed off as fair use.

Example 17: A teacher cuts pictures and articles out of magazines and laminates them. The articles and pictures are kept in a resource file in her classroom. Students consult this file to find information for term papers and oral reports. The file also contains supplemental or incentive reading for pupils who finish their assignments quickly. The teacher uses some of the pictures in name recognition lessons. The laminated pictures and articles will survive several years of heavy use.

Answer: The pictures and articles have not been copied and the pictures have not been publicly displayed (a point treated later in this chapter), so it is unlikely that this is an infringement. This situation should not be confused with the one in Example 10; in that instance consumable materials were laminated to circumvent the single-use limitation. This situation also should not be confused with the one in Example 2; in that instance *photocopies* of articles were placed in a collection. Laminating, rebinding and other methods for preserving copyrighted materials are not illegal unless they are designed to circumvent the single-use provisions for consumable materials.

Example 18: A teacher is writing an individualized instructional unit on a chemical process. An industrial handbook identifies the correct procedure for conducting this process. Failure to follow this process creates a serious hazard. The instructor bases her instructional unit on the procedure in the handbook. The lesson outline generally follows the outline in the handbook; most of the lesson is copied or paraphrased from the handbook. The revisions include changing technical language that might confuse students and expanding a few instructions. The instructional unit will be distributed to students in successive semesters.

Answer: The fact that the information is a substantial copy of a page or two in the handbook and that it will be distributed in multiple copies in successive semesters suggests that it is not a fair use and that permission must be obtained from the publisher. On the other hand, it is not the purpose of copyright to protect ideas, but the expression of ideas. There are many instances in the scientific, technical, and medical fields where a process can, aside from minor changes in the wording, only be expressed in one way. Professor Nimmer comments: "The courts have been inclined to extend the doctrine of fair use, even to permitting a certain amount of word for word similarity, where the matter copied is of a scientific, historical or educational nature."[29] Inasmuch as she did not duplicate the pages, but wrote an instructional unit that inevitably copied the organization and most of the words describing the process, this is a fair use. If the teacher had photocopied the article instead of writing a new unit, then she would have to seek the publisher's permission.

Example 19: A teacher develops a successful new teaching technique. A private educational consulting firm learns about it and asks the teacher to conduct a one-day workshop to explain the technique to other teachers. The teacher is compensated for his expenses and receives a percentage of the profits from the workshop. He develops a packet of materials to distribute to the participants. Two items in the packet are articles reproduced from periodicals. He has never reproduced multiple copies of these articles before, and he does not anticipate doing so again.

Answer: The problem centers on IA in the checklist. The workshop was a for-profit venture, and the participants are paying for the copies through their registration fees. Because of the profit-making nature of this workshop, he should have requested permission to make the copies.

Example 20: A school district professional library acquires single copies of many student workbooks. Most of the workbooks have not been adopted by the district for class use. Teachers browse through the workbooks and photocopy work sheets suitable for their pupils. The photocopies are then duplicated for class use.

Answer: Workbooks are published for class adoption. The work sheets are perforated so the pupils can remove them from the book, complete the work, and submit them to the teacher for grading. They are single-use, consumable materials strictly protected in item IIC. This is an infringement.

Example 21: A teacher has three slow learners in her class. They are often unable to comprehend or complete the work sheets in the adopted workbook. The publisher does not offer a special edition of this workbook for slow learners. The teacher writes some special work sheets for these pupils. She does not have time to do this for every assignment, so she photocopies suitable work sheets from other workbooks for these three pupils.

Answer: Workbooks were purchased for these pupils, so there is apparently no effort to deprive the publisher of a sale (item IVA). The small amount of copying (three copies) from any one item clearly falls within the limits on multiple copying for class distribution (item IC2). The question centers on copying consumable materials. Occasional, spur-of-the-moment copying to help a slow learner may be fair use. However, an organized or systematic effort to copy these consumable materials, even for such a worthy cause, would certainly be an infringement.

Example 22: A teacher ordered standard ability measurement tests for his class. Several students were transferred to the class between the time the order was sent and the examination was given. Additional copies of the test are not available locally, so he made one photocopy of the test for each of the new students.

Answer: Consumable standard examinations are protected from uncleared copying. This part of the law is very strict, but it is not completely inflexible. In this instance, the teacher made an honest effort to purchase enough copies for his class. Making a few copies on short notice in an emergency probably falls within the intent, if not the letter, of the fair use section of the law.

Performance materials

Performance materials are items designed for public performance before an audience. The audience may be in the same room with the performer or scattered throughout the country, listening to the performance on radios or watching it on television sets. Performance materials include sheet music, recorded music, drama, motion picture films, television programs, lectures, and sermons. The owners of these works receive their income from the sale of copies of the work as well as from the sale of performance licenses. Composers derive a small income from the sale of sheet music. The bulk of their income comes from licenses to record the music or to perform it on radio and television stations and in clubs and theaters. Educational film producers derive part of their income from the sale of prints to educational film libraries. Some income comes from the sale of licenses to broadcast the films on instructional television stations. Additional income is derived from selling licenses to school districts that permit them to videotape the films. With the exception of popular music, there is a "thin market" for most of these materials. They are quite vulnerable to unauthorized copying or performances that can deprive the owner of legitimate sales of copies or licenses. The U.S. copyright laws began providing special protection to performance materials in the copyright amendment of 1856. That amendment gave the owners of copyrighted dramatic works the exclusive right to perform the work in public. An actor or producer who wanted to perform the work had to obtain permission, usually with the payment of a fee, from the copyright owner. This concept has been steadily expanded to cover a variety of performance materials. These safeguards include strict limits on copying and on compulsory licenses for certain applications.

Congress resolved the problem of fair use of printed materials by providing the four fair use criteria discussed earlier in this chapter. Those criteria apply, to a limited degree, to performance materials. Congress attempted to resolve the problem of using performance materials in the schools through specific allowances or limitations for each type of material. Some of these limitations and allowances are specified in the law, while others are suggested in the reports.

Face-to-face teaching

The law states that the following are not infringements:

> [P]erformance ... of a work by instructors or pupils in the course of face-to-face teaching activities of a nonprofit educational institution, in a classroom or similar place devoted to instruction, unless, in the case of a motion picture or other audiovisual work, the performance ... is given by means of a copy that was not lawfully made under this title, and that the person responsible for the performance knew or had reason to believe was not lawfully made.[30]

This clearly authorizes a teacher to show a film, filmstrip, videotape, or other audiovisual program, to play a sound recording, to sing a song, or to act out or to have students act out a dramatic performance. The Senate report includes a curious comment about face-to-face teaching:

> [This clause] does not require that the teacher and his students be able to see each other, although it does require their simultaneous presence in the same general place. . . . However, as long as the instructor and pupils are in the same building or general area, the [face-to-face teaching] exemption would extend to the use of devices for amplifying or reproducing sound and for projecting visual images.[31]

This is understood to authorize the use of in-building closed circuit television transmission of films and other audiovisual materials, and the use of in-building sound communications systems to transmit sound recordings. It is specifically limited to the transmission of instructional materials. It is the opinion of at least two attorneys who specialize in these matters that this exemption probably does not apply to transmissions between buildings, even between adjoining buildings on a high school campus. A Copyright Office official recently commented that this element of face-to-face teaching might be stretched to include a single school occupying several buildings, such as a campus-type high school. Clarification may be developed through the courts.

35

Instructional radio and television transmissions

The law states that the following are not infringements:

[P]erformance of a nondramatic literary or musical work . . . by or
in the course of transmission, if—
(A) the performance . . . is a regular part of the systematic
instructional activities of a governmental body or a nonprofit
educational institution; and
(B) the performance . . . is directly related and of material assistance
to the teaching content of the transmission; and
(C) the transmission is made primarily for—
> (i) reception in classrooms or similar places normally devoted to
> instruction, or
> (ii) reception by persons to whom the transmission is directed
> because their disabilities or other special circumstances prevent
> their attendance in classrooms or similar places normally devoted
> to instruction, or
> (iii) reception by officers or employers of governmental bodies
> as a part of their official duties or employment.[32]

The first sentence limits the transmissions to nondramatic
works. Dramatic works include plays, operas, operettas, and
musical comedies. One must obtain permission to transmit these
materials.

The Senate report offers a broad interpretation of subsection A:

The concept of "systematic instructional activities" is intended as the
general equivalent of "curriculums," but it could be broader in a case
such as that of an institution using systematic teaching methods not
related to specific course work. A transmission would be a regular part
of these activities if it is in accordance with the pattern of teaching
established by the governmental body or institution. The use of
commercial facilities, such as those of a cable service, to transmit the
performance or display, would not affect the exemptions as long as
the actual performance or display was for nonprofit purposes.[33]

The report comments on the content of the transmissions discussed in subsection B:

[It] requires that the performance . . . is directly related and of
material assistance to the teaching content of the transmission.[34]

It also expands upon the intended recipients identified in subsection C:

In all three cases, the instructional transmission need only be made "primarily" rather than "solely" to the specified recipients to be exempt. Thus, the transmission could still be exempt even though it is capable of reception by the public at large. Conversely, it would not be regarded as made "primarily" for one of the required groups of recipients if the principal purpose behind the transmission is reception by the public at large, even if it is cast in the form of instruction and is also received in classrooms. Factors to consider in determining the "primary" purpose of a program would include its subject matter, content, and the time of its transmission.

Paragraph (i) . . . generally covers what are known as "in-school" broadcasts, whether open- or closed-circuit. . . . The exemption in paragraph (ii) is intended to exempt transmission providing systematic instruction to individuals who cannot be reached in classrooms because of "their disabilities or other special circumstances." Accordingly, the exemption is confined to instructional broadcasting that is an adjunct to the actual classwork of nonprofit schools or is primarily for people who cannot be brought together in classrooms such as preschool children, displaced workers, illiterates, and shut-ins.

There has been some question as to whether or not the language in this section of the bill is intended to include instructional television college credit courses. These telecourses are aimed at undergraduate and graduate students in earnest pursuit of higher educational degrees who are unable to attend daytime classes due to daytime employment, distance from campus or for some other intervening reason. So long as these broadcasts are aimed at regularly enrolled students and conducted by recognized higher educational institutions, the committee believes that they are clearly within the language of [this section] . . . . [35]

Performances in religious services

Educators in denominational schools should be aware that the law permits a

performance of a nondramatic literary or musical work or of a dramatico-musical work of a religious nature, or display of a work, in the course of services at a place of worship or other religious assembly.[36]

The Senate report expands on this section:

The scope of clause (3) does not cover the sequential showing of motion pictures and other audiovisual works. The exemption . . . applies to dramatico-musical works "of a religious nature." The purpose here is to exempt certain performances of sacred music that might be regarded as "dramatic" in nature, such as oratorios, cantatas, musical settings of the mass, choral services, and the like. The exemption is not intended to cover performances of secular operas, musical plays, motion pictures, and the like, even if they have an underlying religious or philosophical theme and take place "in the course of [religious] services."

To be exempted under [this] section . . . a performance or display must be "in the course of services," thus excluding activities at a place of worship that are for social, educational, fund raising, or entertainment purposes. Some performances of these kinds could be covered by the exemption . . . on benefit performances. . . . Since the performance or display must also occur "at a place of worship or other religious assembly," the exemption would not extend to religious broadcasts or other transmissions to the public at large, even where the transmissions were sent from the place of worship. On the other hand, as long as services are being conducted before a religious gathering, the exemption would apply if they were conducted in places such as auditoriums, outdoor theaters, and the like.[37]

Motion picture films are specifically excluded in the Senate report from the exemption. Some churches use inspirational films in their services. These churches should borrow or rent films under terms that permit this use. Religious film distributors normally permit it. Commercial film distributors often have a special rental rate for the showing of their films in church services.

Benefit performances

The new law permits a

performance of a nondramatic literary or musical work otherwise than in a transmission to the public, without any purpose of direct or indirect commercial advantage and without payment of any fee or other compensation for the performance to any of its performers, promoters, or organizers, if—
A. there is no direct or indirect admission charge; or
B. the proceeds, after deducting the reasonable costs of producing the performance, are used exclusively for educational, religious, or charitable purposes and not for private financial gain, except where the copyright owner has served notice of objection to the performance under the following conditions;
(i) the notice shall be in writing and signed by the copyright owner or such owner's duly authorized agent; and

(ii) the notice shall be served on the person responsible for the performance at least seven days before the date of the performance, and shall state the reasons for the objection; and
(iii) the notice shall comply, in form, content, and manner of service, with requirements that the Register of Copyrights shall prescribe by regulation. . . .[38]

This exemption perpetuates many of the not-for-profit exemptions in the 1909 copyright law. The Senate report indicates that this exemption is

limited to public performances given directly in the presence of an audience whether by means of living performers, the playing of phonorecords, or the operation of a receiving apparatus, and would not include a "transmission to the public. . . ."

No profit motive. – . . . the performance must be "without any purpose of direct or indirect commercial advantage." This provision expressly adopts the principle established by the court decisions construing the "for profit" limitation: that public performances given or sponsored in connection with any commercial or profit-making enterprises are subject to the exclusive rights of the copyright owner even though the public is not charged for seeing or hearing the performance.

No payment for performance. – An important condition for this exemption is that the performance be given "without payment of any fee or other compensation for the performance to any of its performers, promotors, or organizers." The basic purpose of this requirement is to prevent the free use of copyrighted material under the guise of charity where fees or percentages are paid to performers, promotors, producers, and the like. However, the exemption would not be lost if the performers, directors, or producers of the performance, instead of being paid directly "for the performance," are paid a salary for duties encompassing the performance. Examples are performances by a school orchestra conducted by a music teacher who receives an annual salary. . . . The committee believes that performances of this type should be exempt, assuming the other conditions in [this] clause . . . are met. . . .[39]

The House report indicates that the copyright owner's right to prevent the performance of a work in a benefit was included so

the copyright owner is given an opportunity to decide whether and under what conditions the copyrighted work should be performed;

otherwise, owners could be compelled to make involuntary donations to the fund-raising activities of causes to which they are opposed.[40]

This section clears the way for school musical groups to use copyrighted musical works in their performances without paying fees for its use. This only applies to nondramatic music. Dramatic pieces, such as musical comedies, operas, and operettas, are not cleared for public performances. School music directors who wish to perform these pieces must obtain clearances from the copyright owner or the owner's agent.

Transmissions to the blind, deaf, and handicapped

The law permits nonprofit groups to transmit nondramatic literary works (i.e., reading books, magazines, and newspapers) through audio transmissions designed specifically for and directed to the blind and visually handicapped. The transmissions may be transmitted by educational radio and television stations, by radio subcarrier frequencies, or by cable television systems. The transmissions may not be conducted for direct or indirect commercial gain. Nondramatic literary works may also be broadcast through visual transmissions for the deaf and hearing impaired. The same conditions apply to these transmissions.[41]

Dramatic literary works published ten or more years before the performance may be transmitted through radio subcarriers in performances designed for and directed to the blind and visually handicapped. The programs may not be transmitted for direct or indirect commercial gain. A dramatic work may not be performed more than one time for this purpose, by the same performers, or by the same organization.[42]

Reproduction of musical works for classroom use

Voluntary fair use guidelines for copying musical works were developed by representatives of the Music Publishers' Association of the United States, Inc., the National Music Publishers' Association, Inc., the Music Teachers National Association, the Music Educators National Conference, the National Association of Schools of Music, and the Ad Hoc Committee on Copyright Law Revision. The guidelines provide commonsense guidance about duplicating and altering sheet music, for duplicating sound recordings, and for recording student performances.

Sheet music. In an emergency one may duplicate a lost copy that is needed "for an imminent performance." The photocopy should be replaced in due course by a purchased copy. For research purposes other than performance, one may duplicate an excerpt of a work as long as the part duplicated is not a performable unit, such as a selection, movement, or aria. In no instance should the part copied represent more than ten percent of the entire work. Teachers may make multiple copies of a portion of a work for class distribution under the above limitation for research copies and with the customary limitation that the number of copies shall not exceed one per student. Printed copies may be edited or simplified, if the fundamental character of the work is not distorted or the lyrics changed or added.

Sound recordings. A teacher may make a tape recording of sound recordings to construct an aural exercise or examination. The tape may be retained and reused in subsequent terms.

Recording student performances. A single recording of student performances may be produced and retained for evaluation or rehearsal purposes.

The guidelines contain prohibitions against

1. copying to create or replace or substitute for anthologies or collected works.
2. copying consumable materials.
3. copying for the purpose of performance, except for the emergency replacement of a missing piece.
4. copying to avoid purchasing sheet music, except in cases of (a) emergency replacement of a missing piece and (b) need for a small part of a work for teaching or research.
5. omitting the copyright notice from copies.

In examining these guidelines, it is very important to remember that these are *minimum* guidelines. They are reasonable suggestions for the application of fair use, but they *do not* identify the outer limits of fair use copying. In some instances, copying in excess of these guidelines may well be within the limits of fair use. (The complete guidelines text appears in Appendix G.)

Off-air copying of television programs

Modestly priced videotape recorders were introduced in the mid-1960s. By the mid-1970s, many if not most schools had videotape recording equipment. This equipment was commonly used to videotape commercial and educational television broadcasts for later showings in classrooms. Some schools developed large libraries of these recordings. Educators tend to justify it on the grounds that current programs are of great value to teaching. The Columbia Broadcasting System (CBS) actively opposes this practice. In 1973, CBS sued Vanderbilt University for videotaping television news programs, editing the tapes, and making copies for use by scholars. CBS took the position that there can be no fair use copying of their programs. The university filed a countersuit contending that CBS's action was an abridgement of its academic freedom. The two suits were never heard. They were withdrawn in 1976 following the passage of the new copyright law.[43]

The Public Broadcasting Service (PBS) takes a more moderate position. PBS and four of its major producers announced in 1975 that they would permit schools to videotape most of their programs for classroom use on condition that the programs were erased within seven days. (The document is reproduced in Appendix B.) Efforts are now underway to extend this seven-day convenience copying privilege to public library educational programs. A few months after the PBS announcement, the Agency for Instructional Television (AIT) announced that it would permit schools participating in the AIT services to copy and retain AIT programs for one year. (This document is reproduced in Appendix C.)

The Copyright Office worked actively to develop voluntary fair use guidelines for various educational uses of copyrighted materials. The guidelines for music and for printed materials discussed earlier in this chapter were developed as a part of this effort. The Copyright Office also attempted to develop voluntary guidelines for off-air copying of television programs. The interested parties were unable to reach an agreement in time to have it included in the committee reports on the new copyright law. A statement summarizing Congressional thinking appears in the House report:

> The problem of off-the-air taping for nonprofit classroom use of copyrighted audiovisual works incorporated in radio and television broadcasts has proved to be difficult to resolve. The Committee believes that the fair use doctrine has some limited application in this area, but it appears that the development of detailed guidelines will

require a more thorough exploration than has so far been possible of the needs and problems of a number of different interests affected, and of the various legal problems presented. Nothing in section 107 or elsewhere in the bill is intended to change or prejudge the law on the point. On the other hand, the Committee is sensitive to the importance of the problem, and urges the representatives of the various interests, if possible under the leadership of the Register of Copyrights, to continue their discussions actively and in a constructive spirit. If it would be helpful to a solution, the Committee is receptive to undertaking further consideration of the problem in a future Congress.[44]

A meeting of the interested parties was held in July 1977 in an effort to arrive at voluntary guidelines. The meeting was cosponsored by the Copyright Office and the Ford Foundation. The conferees did not arrive at an agreement on this difficult issue. If there had been an agreement, it would not by that time have affected the law. Thus the law does not treat classroom use of copies of television news programs. (One of the documents developed at the conference is reproduced in Appendix E.)

Off-air copying of commercial television *news* programs is clearly permitted. The *CBS* v. *Vanderbilt University* case led to a provision in the law permitting libraries and archives to videotape certain programs. Section 108 states:

Nothing in this section . . . shall be construed to limit the reproduction and distribution by lending of a limited number of copies and excerpts by a library or archive of an audiovisual news program. . . .[45]

The term *audiovisual news program* means televised news broadcasts. The House report expands on this section:

Clause (3) provides that nothing in section 108 is intended to limit the reproduction and distribution by lending of a limited number of copies and excerpts of an audiovisual news program. This exemption is intended to apply to the daily newscasts of the national television networks, which report the major events of the day. It does not apply to documentary (except documentary programs involving news reporting as that term is used in section 107), magazine-format or other public affairs broadcasts dealing with subjects of general interest to the viewing public.

The clause was first added to the revision bill in 1974 by means of an amendment proposed by Senator Baker. It is intended to permit libraries and archives, subject to the general conditions of this section, to make off-the-air videotape recordings of daily network newscasts for limited distribution to scholars and researchers for use in research purposes. As such, it is an adjunct to the American Television and Radio Archive established in Section 113 of the Act which will be the principal repository for the television broadcast material, including news broadcasts. The inclusion of language indicating that such material may only be distributed by lending by the library or archive is intended to preclude performance, copying, or sale, whether or not for profit, by the recipient of a copy of a television broadcast taped off-the-air pursuant to this clause.[46]

The general conditions mentioned in the second paragraph are:

1. [T]he reproduction or distribution is made without any purpose of direct or indirect commercial advantage;
2. the collections of the library or archives are (i) open to the public, or (ii) available not only to researchers affiliated with the library or archives or with the institution of which it is a part, but also to other persons doing research in a specialized field; and
3. the reproduction or distribution of the work includes a notice of copyright.[47]

Educators have asked whether public school libraries could videotape these news programs for class showings. A senior copyright official suggests that this would be acceptable under the above regulations and section 110(a) on performances in face-to-face teaching. A well-known copyright attorney who specializes in copyrights in television programs offers a similar interpretation. The copyright official says the programs should not be transmitted, but should be limited to in-class performances.

The copyright law also permits off-air copying of Presidential addresses and Congressional hearings. The law generally denies copyright protection to government publications. Works published without copyright protection are said to be in the public domain, and anyone may copy them freely and exploit them in almost any way. As a result, educators are free to videotape Presidential addresses and Congressional hearings for repeated class use. Almost all of these programs are followed by a commentary by network newscasters. Some attorneys regard these segments as copyrighted materials which may not be videotaped. One senior copyright official identifies these commentaries as "on-the-spot news coverage" which may be videotaped by libraries and archives under the terms of section 108(f)(3). This interpretation has a certain logic to it.

A last-minute addition to the commentaries on the copyright bill suggests that fair use may be interpreted to give schools for the deaf some latitude in videotaping television programs and to add captions from the sound tracks for the benefit of the deaf and hearing impaired. This suggestion is found in Representative Kastenmeier's comments on the floor of the House:

> Also in consultation with section 107, the committee's attention has been directed to the unique educational needs and problems of the approximately 50,000 deaf and hearing-impaired students in the United States, and the inadequacy of both public and commercial television to serve their educational needs. It has been suggested that, as long as clear-cut constraints are imposed and enforced, the doctrine of fair use is broad enough to permit the making of an off-the-air fixation of a television program within a nonprofit educational institution for the deaf and hearing impaired, the reproduction of a master and a work copy of a captioned version of the original fixation, and the performance of the program from the work copy within the confines of the institution. In identifying the constraints that would have to be imposed within an institution in order for these activities to be considered as fair use, it has been suggested that the purpose of the use would have to be noncommercial in every respect, and educational in the sense that it serves as part of a deaf or hearing-impaired student's learning environment within the institution, and that the institution would have to insure that the master and work copy would remain in the hands of a limited number of authorized personnel within the institution, would be responsible for assuring against its unauthorized reproduction or distribution, or its performance or retention for other than educational purposes within the institution. Work copies of captioned programs could be shared among institutions for the deaf abiding by the constraints specified. Assuming that these constraints are both imposed and enforced, and that no other factors intervene to render the use unfair, the committee believes that the activities described could reasonably be considered fair use under section 107.[48]

Representative Kastenmeier chairs the House Subcommittee on the Courts, Civil Liberties, and the Administration of Justice. The subcommittee conducted the hearings on the copyright bill. The report of the Conference Committee sustained Representative Kastenmeier's statement.[49]

Classroom performances of dramatic literary and musical works

It has been noted before that dramatic works are closely protected by the new copyright law. Dramatic works include plays, operas, operettas, and musical comedies. Section 110(a), on face-to-face teaching, permits a teacher or student to perform all or part of a dramatic work without the permission of the copyright owner. This includes, but is not limited to, performing plays in a drama class, performing plays in a preschool class, performing operatic pieces in a voice class, or performing selections from a musical comedy in an instrumental music class. Attendance at these performances must be limited to the pupils enrolled in the class and the instructional personnel assigned to the room. Instructional personnel would include the teachers or teaching team and paid or volunteer aides. The performance may take place in a classroom, studio, auditorium, gymnasium, or any other place appropriate to the instructional process, as long as the attendance limitations are met. Performances before larger audiences (with or without an admission fee) do not conform to these limitations. Permission must be obtained for these performances.

Preservation of out-of-print materials

The Senate report states that fair use applies to making complete copies of performance materials for the purpose of preserving them for future use. The efforts of the Library of Congress and the American Film Institute to preserve pre-1942 motion picture films printed on nitrate stock are given as examples of this application. The photocopying section of the law has a similar provision:

> The right of reproduction under this section applies to a copy or phonorecord of a published work duplicated in facsimile form solely for the purpose of replacement of a copy or phonorecord that is damaged, deteriorating, lost, or stolen, if the library or archives has, after a reasonable effort, determined that an unused replacement cannot be obtained at a fair price.[50]

The House report adds that the search for a replacement copy

> will always require recourse to commonly-known trade sources in the United States, and in the normal situation also to the publisher or

other copyright owner (if such owner can be located at the address listed in the copyright registration), or an authorized reproducing service.[51]

Although the law and the report speak only of reproducing copies that are damaged, deteriorating, lost, or stolen, it seems reasonable to apply this to old television programs recorded on the older, nonstandardized equipment formats. The manufacturers stopped making these machines years ago, and it is becoming increasingly difficult to keep these old machines operating. When replacement parts are no longer available, then it will be impossible to service them. Out-of-print programs that are only available on these formats must be copied to preserve them. Fair use certainly seems to apply to this situation.

Format changes that do not require copying

Neither the law nor the committee report has a provision for format changes that do not require copying. Representatives of educational media producers indicate that it is usually acceptable to convert a filmstrip to a slide set, if by so doing the program is more useful. This is only acceptable if the program retains its integrity and identity. It cannot be edited to say something the producer did not intend to say. It cannot be expanded by adding content or abridged by deleting part of the content. An alteration to the content creates a derivative work and fair use does not apply to the creation of derivative works.

There is also a general agreement that one may cut a small number of frames out of a filmstrip and remount them in slide frames for use in other educational applications. The fair use criteria suggest that one may copy a small part of a work for class use. This would also seem to permit removing and remounting a small number of frames as an alternative to copying them. It is important to remember, though, that filmstrips are performance materials and only a small amount may be copied or removed for other uses.

Ephemeral recordings

Section 112 of the copyright law introduces a new form of users' rights borrowed from the copyright laws of some European countries. Ephemeral recordings are made by radio and television stations to facilitate the editing of programs. The successive parts of a program are prerecorded on audiotape or videotape, and the tape is then played for the transmission.

Two parts of this section relate to schools and libraries. *Instructional broadcasting.* It is permissible for

a governmental body or other nonprofit organization entitled to transmit a performance or display of a work, under section 110(2) or under the limitations on exclusive rights in sound recordings specified by section 114(a), to make no more than thirty copies or phonorecords of a particular transmission program embodying the performance or display, if—
(1) no further copies or phonorecords are reproduced from the copies or phonorecords made under this clause; and
(2) except for one copy or phonorecord that may be preserved exclusively for archival purposes, the copies or phonorecords are destroyed within seven years from the date the transmission program was first transmitted to the public.[52]

The Senate report comments:

[This] represents a response to the arguments of educational broadcasters and other educational groups for special recording privileges, although it does not go as far as these groups requested. In general, it permits a nonprofit organization that is free to transmit a performance or display of a work, under section 110(2) [instructional transmissions] . . . to make not more than thirty copies or phonorecords and to use the ephemeral recordings for transmitting purposes for not more than seven years after the initial transmission.[53]

The law has somewhat vague definitions of transmissions and transmission programs:

A "transmission program" is a body of material that, as an aggregate, has been produced for the sole purpose of transmission to the public in sequence and as a unit.

To "transmit" a performance or display is to communicate it by any device or process whereby images or sounds are received beyond the place from which they are sent.[54]

At this point it would seem that the right to make ephemeral recordings applies to any educational institution engaged in transmitting instructional programs via cable or broadcast. The Senate report continues its explanation:

Scope of the privilege. – Under subsection (b) an instructional *broadcaster* [emphasis added] may make "no more than thirty copies of phonorecords of a particular transmission program embodying the performance of display."[55]

Notice that the report uses the term "instructional broadcaster." The law does not define broadcaster or instructional broadcaster, but it does provide for compulsory licenses "in connection with noncommercial broadcasting."[56] The House report on this section speaks of requiring the payment of licenses for "transmissions by noncommercial educational broadcast stations. . . ."[57] The law and the committee reports are certainly not as clear as they should be in identifying agencies entitled to the benefits of the ephemeral recording section. However, when the ephemeral recording section and the compulsory license section are read together, it appears that the ephemeral recording section applies only to those broadcasters covered by the compulsory license requirements. The Senate report adds an additional comment:

> No further copies or phonorecords can be reproduced from those made under section 112(b), either by the nonprofit organization that made them or by anyone else. Unlike ephemeral recordings made [by commercial broadcasting stations] . . . exchanges of recordings among instructional broadcasters are permitted. An organization that has made copies or phonorecords under subsection (b) may use one of them for purposes of its own transmissions that are exempted by section 110(2) [i.e., instructional broadcasting], and it may also transfer the other 29 copies to other instructional broadcasters for use in the same way.
>
> As in the case of ephemeral recordings made [by a commercial broadcaster] . . . a copy or phonorecord made for instructional broadcasting could be reused in any number of transmissions within the time limits specified in the provision. Because of the special problems of instructional broadcasters resulting from the scheduling of courses and the need to prerecord well in advance of transmission, the period of use has been extended to seven years from the date the transmission program was first transmitted to the public.[58]

This complicated matter may be summarized as follows:

1. The ephemeral recording privilege only applies to instructional broadcasters who pay the compulsory licensing fee. (The author interprets this point conservatively; some author-

ities contend that the ephemeral recording right applies to all instructional transmissions identified in section 110(2).)

2. These broadcasters may make up to thirty copies of copyrighted audio and display materials for inclusion in their programs.
3. The thirty copies may be retained for up to seven years. One copy may be retained indefinitely for archival purposes.
4. The copies may be exchanged with other instructional broadcasters.
5. Both the producing station and the stations receiving exchange copies may transmit the programs. They may be transmitted repeatedly during the seven-year period.
6. Unlicensed individuals and agencies may not copy the programs.
7. The impreciseness of the law and the lack of clear-cut guidance in the committee reports suggest that this matter will have to be clarified through expensive litigation. Prudence is recommended.

Transmission to the blind, deaf, and handicapped. Section 112(d) permits organizations authorized to transmit nondramatic literary works (see an earlier section of this chapter entitled: "Transmissions to the Blind, Deaf, and Handicapped," page 40) to make up to ten copies of the performances. They may permit other authorized transmitting organizations to transmit the copies. The copies may be kept indefinitely.[59]

Other uses

Other fair use copying from performance materials must be determined by applying the fair use criteria and their subsections. Subsection IID of the fair use checklist indicates that fair use applies in a lesser degree to performance materials. The Senate report elaborates on this difference:

> The character and purpose of the work will have a lot to do with whether its reproduction for classroom purposes is fair use or infringement. For example, in determining whether a teacher could make one or more copies without permission, a news article from the daily press would be judged differently from a full orchestral score of a musical composition. In general terms it could be expected that the doctrine of fair use would be applied strictly to the classroom reproduction of entire works, such as musical compositions, dramas,

and audiovisual works including motion pictures, which by their nature are intended for performance or public exhibition.[60]

Fair use by nonclassroom educators

To judge from the language of the committee reports, the fair use section appears to have been written for the benefit of classroom teachers. Nonclassroom educators (administrators, curriculum specialists, counselors, media specialists, librarians, instructional designers, and so on) seem to be overlooked in the reports. Representative Robert W. Kastenmeier clarified the matter when he presented the bill for debate on the floor of the House: "[T]he committee regards the concept of 'teacher' as broad enough to include instructional specialists working in consultation with actual instructors."[61] His statement is sustained in the report of the Conference Committee.[62] When a specialist works in collaboration with a teacher to locate or produce learning materials, then the specialist has the same privileges a teacher would have. This does not permit a specialist or an administrator to direct a teacher to make the copies or to make the copies and direct a teacher to distribute them. Nonclassroom educators only have the teacher's broad rights when they are working in close collaboration with a teacher.

Examples: Duplicating performance materials

Example 1: A school prepares a nonbroadcast instructional television program. The program requires a tropical vegetation scene. The producer locates an eighty-second scene in a 16mm instructional film and copies the visual portion. The scene represents about nine percent of the running time of the film and about five percent of the running time of the television program. This is the only copyrighted material included in the television program.

Answer: The question can be worked out using the fair use checklist. (Readers may want to use a photocopy of the checklist to follow along with the explanation.) Part A of the first criterion applies to this situation; the program is made by and for a nonprofit school and there will be no charge to see the program. Part IB1 is clearly met. The program was made by a team of instructional specialists who produced it in response to a teacher's request and with the intent that the program will be used in the teacher's class. This clearly fits the "Kastenmeier rule" discussed in the preceding section. Part IB2 does not create a problem. Although the teacher or the television producer might have time to seek permission, they are not required to do so if the remaining fair use criteria are met. Item IC is satisfied if only one copy is made. The important question occurs in criterion IID. A film is a performance material that is closely protected by the law. As long as (1) the amount of copying is small in relation to the length of the film, (2) the section that is copied is not exceptionally valuable footage which would be difficult, if not impossible, to reproduce, and (3) the portion copied represents a small part of the finished instructional product, then it is probably fair use *if the other criteria are met.* The fourth criterion must be carefully considered. If the copying, directly or indirectly, replaces a sale, then it is not a fair use. Some film producers now offer licenses to reproduce scenes from their films. One major educational film producer now issues an encyclopedia of scenes, which they sell to instructional film and television producers. Any copying that replaces the sale of one of these scenes is clearly an infringement under the fourth criterion, regardless of how successfully it meets the other criteria.

Example 2: A library finds that children are very careless in handling phonograph records. Many records are badly damaged after a few circulations. The library makes one cassette copy of each record. The records are retained in a noncirculating master collection, and the cassette copies are circulated. If a tape is damaged or lost, another copy can be made in a few hours without purchasing a new record.

Answer: The fourth criterion prevents this type of copying. If the recording is available on the market, then making a copy deprives the producer of a legitimate sale. The action is an infringement. If unused copies of the recording are no longer available at a reasonable price, then the exemption for preserving out-of-print materials permits making a single copy to preserve the content. The problem of replacing damaged or missing sound recordings is complicated by the fact that many record titles are only available for a short time and then they are withdrawn from the market. One library recently developed a policy designed to observe the spirit of the law without losing easy access to out-of-print recordings. All records are duplicated when they arrive, and the tapes are held in a noncirculating master collection. If the phonograph record is lost or damaged, the library attempts to purchase a replacement copy. If an unused copy of the record cannot be purchased through the normal trade sources at a "reasonable price," the library makes a cassette copy of the master tape. The cassette copy is circulated in the usual manner, and the master tape is returned to the noncirculating master file. If the cassette copy is lost or damaged, the library again attempts to buy a replacement copy of the recording (in either cassette or disc format). If an unused copy is not available at a "reasonable price," another cassette copy is made from the master. This appears to be fair use.

Example 3: A teacher shows a number of films in her film study class each semester. The films are rented, and they are usually available for only one day. The teacher asks the media center to reproduce several key frames from each film. The frames are duplicated onto slides. The slides are then used in class for review and discussion of the film.

Answer: This clearly falls within the intent of the fair use section on copying for the purpose of criticism. The amount of film copied was slight. This seems to be a fair use.

Example 4: A university film study instructor also has copies made of selected frames of the films used in his class. The copies are to be placed in the library for independent study by students enrolled in the class. The library does not have slide projectors or viewers, so the slides are reproduced on microfiche.

Answer: The fact that the film frames had to be duplicated onto slides and then onto microfiche was dictated by the limits of the available technology. It remains a duplication of a small part of the work for the purpose of criticism. It seems to be a fair use.

Example 5: Students in an audiovisual production class are assigned to make a slide program with narration. They are required to mix music with the narration at the opening and closing of the program. Some students use copyrighted music for this purpose.

Answer: Item IE in the checklist reminds us that Congress intended fair use to apply with greater latitude to copying by students, when the copying was done to acquire mastery in the given unit of study. As long as the programs remain the students' personal property and are not used for commercial gain, this seems to be a fair use.

Example 6: A media center produces a sound-slide instructional program for a teacher. Only one copy is made. The program includes brief segments of background music at the beginning and the end of the program. The music is copyrighted.

Answer: Although this is performance material, the small amount copied might fit within the bounds of fair use, if it is done infrequently. If the media center produces many programs for which they supply background music, they should acquire "cleared music." (Cleared music is discussed in chapter 4, pages 99-102.)

Example 7: A music teacher arranged to have a technician record short extracts from several pieces of copyrighted music, along with the teacher's recorded explanation of each selection. Several cassette copies are made for individual use by students.

Answer: In this instance, the amount of copying from any given selection was small. The first problem appears to occur when these small segments are gathered into a single anthology. The "Guidelines for Educational Uses of Music" in the House report suggest that

a single copy of a sound recording (such as a tape, disc, or cassette) of copyrighted music may be made from sound recordings owned by an educational institution or an individual teacher for the purpose of constructing aural exercises or examinations and may be retained by the educational institution or individual teacher.[63]

This only applies if it does not "create or replace or substitute for anthologies, compilations or collective works."[64] The second problem in this example is the duplication of multiple copies of the recording. That clearly falls outside the "single copy" limitation of these *minimum* guidelines. It appears that the original tape recording is a fair use; making a few additional cassette copies to accommodate a large class may fall within the limits of fair use.

Example 8: A library has a collection of sound filmstrips with the sound tracks on disc recordings. The library's last turntable model sound filmstrip machine is worn-out, and they want to convert the disc format sound filmstrips to the newer cassette format. The disc recordings are duplicated onto cassettes.

Answer: Most producers of sound filmstrips offer sound filmstrips in both audio formats. Some producers recognize this problem and sell cassette tapes as a separate item (i.e., without the other components) for libraries wanting to make the conversion. Making a copy without permission duplicates a large part of a copyrighted work and may result in the loss of a sale. It is an infringement. Libraries that want to make this conversion should draft a form letter requesting permission to convert the existing sound filmstrips from the disc format to the cassette format. The letter should be sent to each of the producers. The producer then has two reasonable options; either grant permission, or offer to sell the cassette copies. The economic recession in the educational media field has forced some producers out of business. If a producer has gone out of business and cannot be reached at the firm's latest known address, then the record could be copied without permission. The library's efforts to reach the producer would show evidence of good faith in the event that questions are raised about the copying.

Example 9: A school has a 16mm film they want children to use as an individualized study item. The children can operate a videocassette playback machine, but they are too young to safely operate a 16mm projector. The film is videotaped for this purpose.

Answer: A performance material is copied in its entirety. That alone is a copyright infringement. In addition, almost all educational filmmakers offer licenses to copy their films onto videotape. Making an unlicensed copy deprives them of a legitimate sale.

Example 10: A school purchases large numbers of sound filmstrips. They prefer to have the audio portion in the cassette format. They notice that most producers offer sound filmstrips in both the disc and cassette formats, but that the disc format programs are sometimes cheaper than the same program in the cassette format. They purchase the programs in the cheaper disc format and have volunteers transfer the audio portion onto cassettes.

Answer: It is uncertain whether this affects the producer's profits, but it obviously involves a systematic duplication of copyrighted materials, and thus is an infringement.

Example 11: A teacher uses many slides in his lectures. He finds an old filmstrip that has been damaged and will be discarded. He locates several undamaged frames that would be useful for his lectures. He removes the frames and mounts them in slide frames. They are mixed with his other slides. *Answer:* This should be considered in the same light as copying a small number of frames and incorporating them in other materials. Reusing a small number of frames seems acceptable, but reusing all or almost all of the frames would be an infringement.

Example 12: A school prefers to use sound-slide viewers for individual use by students. Some sound filmstrips are cut apart and the frames are mounted in slide frames. The content is not altered.

Answer: Industry representatives regard this as a fair use, as long as the content is not changed.

Example 13: A school has a dial-access facility that uses a four-track, random access, monaural audio tape system. The school cannot purchase many recordings in this format, so they duplicate the recordings onto the required format. The original recordings are retained in a noncirculating master file.

Answer: Copying a work to change its format is normally regarded as an infringement. However, educational media producers generally view this as an acceptable practice. The owners of musical copyrights do not approve of any reproduction of their materials. It might be advisable to use purchase order specifications, described in chapter 4, pages 102-3, to obtain permission to make these copies.

Example 14: A special education teacher makes a new sound track for a sound filmstrip appropriate to the vocabulary level of the slow learners in her class. Only one copy of the new sound track is made; it will be used for several years.

Answer: This constitutes a major change in the intellectual content of the sound filmstrip. It creates a derivative work, which is an infringement. If a filmstrip or a special sound track for slow learners is not available, the teacher should write to the producer for permission to make the special sound track. If the producers begin receiving requests for permission to make this type of adaptation, it is quite possible that they will begin producing appropriate programs or special sound tracks for this audience.

Display materials

A major change in the law recognizes an author's right to display his or her works. This right appears in the list of exclusive rights:

[T]he owner of copyright under this title has the exclusive right to do and to authorize any of the following:

. . .

(5) in the case of literary, musical, dramatic, and choreographic works, pantomimes, and pictorial, graphic, or sculptural works, including the individual images of a motion picture or other audiovisual work, to display the work publicly.[65]

The Senate report explains this new right:

[This section] represents the first explicit statutory recognition in American copyright law of an exclusive right to show a copyrighted work, or an image of it, to the public.[66]

And further:

The . . . definition of "display" covers any showing of a "copy" of the work, "either directly or by means of a film, slide, television image, or any other device or process." Since "copies" are defined as including the material object "in which the work is first fixed," the right of public display applies to original works of art as well as to reproductions of them. . . . In addition to the direct showings of a copy of a work, "display" would include the projection of an image on a screen or other surface by any method, the transmission of an image by electronic or other means, and the showing of an image on a cathode ray tube, or similar viewing apparatus connected with any sort of information storage and retrieval system.

> Under . . . the definition of "publicly," a . . . display is "public" if it takes place "at a place open to the public or at any place where a substantial number of persons outside of a normal circle of a family and its social acquaintances is gathered.". . . . Routine meetings of business and governmental personnel would be excluded because they do not represent the gathering of a "substantial number of persons."[67]

The law defines display materials as:

> "Pictorial, graphic, and sculptural works" including two-dimensional and three-dimensional works of fine, graphic, and applied art, photographs, prints and art reproductions, maps, globes, charts, technical drawings, diagrams, and models. Such works shall include works of artistic craftsmanship insofar as their form but not their mechanical or utilitarian aspects are concerned; . . .[68]

This new aspect of copyright permits an artist or craftsman to regulate public showings of his or her paintings, photographs, prints, pottery, and the like. If the creator does not want to have a work displayed, he or she has a right to prevent it from being shown, providing the creator did not previously convey the right to display the work. The conveyance may have been granted (in writing) at the time of the sale of the work, or in a separate transaction. If the creator still holds the display rights, he or she may regulate the manner in which it is shown and he or she can require a fee payment for the showing. Any individual or institution that publicly displays these works improperly infringes the creator's copyright. This poses obvious problems for public libraries and educational institutions. Most of these problems are resolved in the law and the accompanying reports. Sections 109 and 110 offer several exemptions:

Public display by the owner

Section 109 of the law offers the following exemption:

> Notwithstanding the provisions of section 106(5), the owner of a particular copy lawfully made under this title, or any person authorized by such owner, is entitled, without the authority of the copyright owner, to display that copy publicly, either directly or by the projection of no more than one image at a time, to viewers present at the place where the copy is located.
>   The privileges prescribed [above] . . . do not, unless authorized by the copyright owner, extend to any person who has acquired

possession of the copy or phonorecord from the copyright owner, by rental, lease, loan, or otherwise, without acquiring ownership of it.[69]

The first paragraph permits schools and libraries to publicly display art works and the like. It does not permit them to transmit the materials for showing at another place. The second paragraph gives copyright owners and their agents the right to regulate public displays of display materials that are rented, leased, or loaned. This permits film distributors to regulate the showings of their films. Some educational film distributors, such as Time-Life Films, do not sell copies of their films. They sell life-of-the-print leases for their films. This permits these firms to stipulate the manner in which the films are used. If a film is used in an unauthorized manner, the firm can seize the film. This also applies to films rented from educational, religious, and commercial film rental libraries. If the person or agency renting the film uses it in an unauthorized manner, they may be prosecuted for the action. This section does not significantly alter existing practices, it just augments existing contractual agreements with the force of the copyright law.

Displays in face-to-face teaching

The exemption in section 109 is extended in section 110, which indicates the following are not infringements:

> [D]isplay of a work by instructors or pupils in the course of face-to-face teaching activities of a nonprofit educational institution, in a classroom or similar place devoted to instruction, unless, in the case of a motion picture or other audiovisual work, the . . . display of individual images, is given by means of a copy that was not lawfully made under this title, and that the person responsible for the . . . [display] knew or had reason to believe was not lawfully made.[70]

Displays via instructional radio and television transmissions

The law states that the following are not infringements:

> [The] display of a work, by or in the course of a transmission, if—

A. the . . . display is a regular part of the systematic instructional activities of a governmental body or a nonprofit educational institution; and

B. the . . . display is directly related and of material assistance to the teaching content of the transmission; and

C. the transmission is made primarily for—

(i) reception in classrooms or similar places normally devoted to instruction, or

(ii) reception by persons to whom the transmission is directed because their disabilities or other special circumstances prevent their attendance in classrooms or similar places normally devoted to instruction, or

(iii) reception by officers or employees of governmental bodies as a part of their official duties or employment.[71]

This provision is discussed at length on page 36.

Reproduction of display materials

The law and the reports offer little guidance for the application of fair use copying to display materials. The Agreement on Guidelines suggests the minimum for fair use copying should be "one chart, graph, diagram, drawing, cartoon, or picture per book or per periodical issue."[72] These guidelines are acknowledged by their authors as minimum guidelines. This particular part of the guidelines is especially hard to apply. Some books and periodicals have few illustrations, while others consist chiefly of illustrations. Until Congress or the courts offer better guidance in this matter, it may be safe to assume that fair use permits reproducing a single copy of a small part of a work for personal use or multiple copies of a small part of a work for class distribution. To apply fair use, one must determine the extent of the protection of the work by examining the copyright notice. Three patterns of copyright protection are commonly found for these works: (1) Individual copyright protection for each picture or graphic. A few publishers place a separate copyright on each photograph or other illustration appearing in their books or magazines. (2) A single copyright for a set of works (e.g., a set of four photographs in a magazine protected by a single copyright). (3) A single copyright for all of the textual, graphic, and photographic matter in the book or article.

The new copyright law no longer requires that separately copyrighted works (articles, photographs, cartoons) appearing in a collective work (book, magazine) display a separate copyright notice. Under these circumstances it is sometimes difficult to know which of these levels of copyright protection apply to a photograph or illustration. Fortunately, the new law permits making copying decisions on the basis of the available evidence (copyright notices). Copyright notices frequently appear in the margin of photographic and graphic works. They sometimes appear in the credits section of periodicals and books. The notice may also appear next to the copyright notice for the entire book, periodical, or audiovisual program. If a separate copyright notice cannot be found for illustrations, they are probably protected by the copyright for the entire book, periodical, or audiovisual program.

If a single photograph or graphic is copyrighted as a separate work, then the fair use guidelines probably only permit copying a small part of it. If a number of photographs or graphics are protected by a single copyright notice, then the fair use guidelines probably permit copying a small part of the set. The law treats display materials much like performance materials, suggesting that they are closely protected. Copying in excess of a small amount should only be done with the permission of the copyright owner. The copyright owners for photographs are often hard to identify and locate. A recently published book, *Stock Photo and Assignment Source Book* by F. W. McDarrah, may be useful for this purpose.[73]

 **Library
photocopying**

Photocopying of copyrighted materials by library personnel grew slowly before World War II. By present standards, the equipment was crude and expensive, effectively limiting the number of copies that could be made. Questions were soon raised though about copyright infringements resulting from the use of these machines. A voluntary and nonbinding agreement, the Gentlemen's Agreement of 1937, was developed by three interested parties: The Joint Committee on Materials for Research of the American Council of Learned Societies, the Social Science Research Council, and the Association of Book Publishers. The last named association did not represent many publishers, especially publishers of scientific and technical journals. It is no longer in existence. Congress attempted to resolve the problem through two copyright revision bills, the Shotwell Bill of 1940 and the Lucas Bill of 1944. Neither bill passed. The problem was aggravated by the introduction of fast, simple, and inexpensive copying machines in the 1960s.

The controversy centered on photocopying journal articles for interlibrary loan. The issue was brought to a head when the publishing firm of Williams & Wilkins sued the National Institutes of Health (NIH) and the National Library of Medicine

(NLM) for infringing the firm's copyrights in six of their medical journals. The NLM has a substantial collection of medical journals. Articles are photocopied from these journals in response to requests from researchers at the NIH and in response to interlibrary loan requests. The suit finally reached the Supreme Court. The Supreme Court voted a 4-4 split, with Justice Blackmun abstaining. Nimmer conjectures that if Justice Blackmun had voted, he would have voted in favor of the publisher.[1] The decision of the Supreme Court sustained the narrow 4-3 decision in the Court of Claims without setting a precedent. The decision of the Court of Claims favored the NIH/NLM. Flacks comments: "This is very interesting, but considering the narrowness of the Court of Claims decision, it is doubtful whether such a highly technical argument is terribly important in the long run." He then sums up the feelings of many of those who have studied the case: "Regardless of how hard one hacks away at Williams and Wilkins, it's still there in the morning."[2]

The broad and somewhat generalized exemptions of the fair use section are often difficult to apply to library photocopying. Clearer answers are found in section 108 which provides specific applications of the fair use concept to library photocopying. Section 108 is long and complicated, and its arrangement can be baffling. In an effort to bring order to this sometimes confusing section, this chapter is arranged in two parts. It begins by identifying ten basic elements or requirements that can be distilled from section 108. It is followed by an application of section 108 to types of materials and types of services (e.g., copying in-print materials and copying for interlibrary loan services). In reading the ten basic requirements, remember that they are indeed *general* requirements, and some of them do not apply to every situation. The exceptions are identified in the treatment of specific materials and services.

The ten basic requirements

1. Photocopies are made and distributed without direct or indirect commercial advantage.
2. The collection is open to the public or open to researchers from outside the sponsoring firm or institution.
3. The reproduction includes a copyright notice.
4. Copying is limited to a single copy of an article from a periodical or to a small part of other works.

5. The copy remains the property of the patron for his or her private study or research.
6. The library displays a notice at each self-service copying machine and at the place where orders are taken for copies. The notice must also appear on copying request forms.
7. A library cannot knowingly help a patron copy a large part of a work or make multiple copies of a part of a work by means of single or repeated copying.
8. A library may not enter into arrangements for the systematic duplication of single or multiple copies of a work.
9. The copyright law does not affect "contractual obligations assumed at any time by the library or archives when it obtained a copy or phonorecord of a work in its collections."[3]
10. With certain exceptions, a library may not reproduce or distribute copies of musical, pictorial, graphic, sculptural, or audiovisual works.

The first requirement states: "[T]he reproduction or distribution is made without any purpose of direct or indirect commercial advantage. . . ."[4] The House of Representatives committee report comments:

> Under this provision, a purely commercial enterprise could not establish a collection of copyrighted works, call itself a library or archive, and engage in for-profit reproduction and distribution of photocopies. Similarly, it would not be possible for a non-profit institution, by means of contractual arrangements with a commercial copying enterprise, to authorize the enterprise to carry out copying and distribution functions that would be exempt if conducted by the non-profit institution itself.[5]

The last part of the sentence causes some librarians to wonder if it was meant to prevent libraries from leasing commercially owned photocopying machines. This point is not clear in the law or reports, but it is widely believed that it was not intended to prevent this practice. It was probably designed to prevent libraries from introducing commercial, for-profit copying services in the library. A small number of libraries have given or leased space in the library to a commercial copying firm to relieve the library of this responsibility. The law seems to be directed at preventing this practice. The writer knows of one university library that prices its staff-operated copying service at two cents per sheet above the cost of operating the service. The two-cents-per-sheet profit is allocated to the library's office supply fund. The writer is not prepared to say that this is illegal, but he suspects that it falls outside the intent of the not-for-profit concept.

This section of the law raises special problems for libraries operated by for-profit firms. The House report comments at length on this problem.

> The reference to "indirect commercial advantage" has raised questions as to the status of photocopying done by or for libraries or archival collections within industrial, profit-making, or proprietary institutions (such as the research and development departments of chemical, pharmaceutical, automobile, and oil corporations, the library of a proprietary hospital, the collections owned by a law or medical partnership, etc.).
>
> There is a direct interrelationship between this problem and the prohibitions against "multiple" and "systematic" photocopying in section 108(g)(1) and (2). Under section 108, a library in a profit-making organization would not be authorized to:
> (a) use a single subscription or copy to supply its employees with multiple copies of material relevant to their work; or
> (b) use a single subscription or copy to supply its employees, on request, with single copies of material relevant to their work, where the arrangement is "systematic" in the sense of deliberately substituting photocopying for subscriptions or purchases; or
> (c) use "interlibrary loan" arrangements for obtaining photocopies in such aggregate quantities as to substitute for subscriptions or purchase of material needed by employees in their work.
>
> Moreover, a library in a profit-making organization could not evade these obligations by installing reproducing equipment on its premises for unsupervised use by the organization's staff.
>
> Isolated, spontaneous making of single photocopies by a library in a for-profit organization, without any systematic effort to substitute photocopying for subscriptions or purchases, would be covered by section 108, even though the copies are furnished to the employees of the organization for use in their work. Similarly, for-profit libraries could participate in interlibrary arrangements for exchange of photocopies, as long as the reproduction or distribution was not "systematic." These activities, by themselves, would ordinarily not be considered "for direct or indirect commercial advantage," since the "advantage" referred to in this clause must attach to the immediate commercial motivation behind the reproduction or distribution itself, rather than to the ultimate profit-making motivation behind the

enterprise in which the library is located. On the other hand, section 108 would not excuse reproduction or distribution if there was a commercial motive behind the actual making or distributing of the copies, if multiple copies were made or distributed, or if the photocopying activities were "systematic" in the sense that their aim was to substitute for subscriptions or purchases.[6]

The second requirement reads:

[T]he collections of the library or archives are (*i*) open to the public, or (*ii*) available not only to researchers affiliated with the library or archives or with the institution of which it is a part, but also to other persons doing research in a specialized field. . . .[7]

There is little question about the first part. Any library that is open to the public complies with this requirement. The second part refers to special libraries in for-profit organizations. If the special library is "available" to (1) researchers from other firms, (2) students and professors conducting research, and (3) independent researchers, then it appears to comply with the requirement. The library can place some limitations on the use of the collection by persons outside the firm, as long as the collection is "available" to them.

The third requirement states, "[T]he reproduction or distribution of the work includes a notice of copyright."[8] Some printed materials have a copyright notice appearing at the bottom of each page or on the first page of each article. This notice should be reproduced in the photocopy. If a copyright notice does not appear in the part being copied, then the library must supply some form of notice. The Interlibrary Loan Committee of the American Library Association's Reference and Adult Services Division *recommends* that the following notice be placed on the copy: "Notice: This material may be protected by copyright law (Title 17 U.S. Code)."[9] Some photocopying machines may be equipped to print this statement on copies; if not, the notice can be added by means of a rubber stamp or an adhesive label. Some libraries reproduce the copyright notice (found on the title page verso) on the first page of the photocopy. This practice is quite acceptable.

The fourth, fifth, and sixth requirements are listed in section 108(d). The fourth requirement states that single copies may be made only of a *small part* of a work:

The rights of reproduction and distribution under this section apply to a copy made from the collection of a library or archives where the user makes his or her request or from that of another library or archives, of no more than one article or other contribution to a copyrighted collection or periodical issue, or to a copy or phonorecord of a small part of any other copyrighted work....[10]

This is immediately followed by a fifth requirement about the ownership and use of the copy:

[T]he copy or phonorecord becomes the property of the user, and the library or archives has had no notice that the copy or phonorecord would be used for any purpose other than private study, scholarship, or research....[11]

If a library staff member has reason to believe that the copy will be used for purposes other than private study, scholarship, or research, then the copy should not be made. This does not suggest that libraries must inquire about the intended use. It would seem to be sufficient to be alert to a patron's comments that might suggest an illegal use of the copy. The requirement that the copy must remain the user's personal property appears to forbid the common practice of placing photocopies of articles in library pamphlet files.

The sixth requirement specifies that copyright warning signs must be posted at appropriate places:

[T]he library or archives displays prominently, at the place where orders are accepted, and includes in its order form, a warning of copyright in accordance with requirements that the Register of Copyrights shall prescribe by regulation.[12]

On November 10, 1977, the Copyright Office issued a regulation requiring libraries and archives to display the notice shown in figure 2 in places where orders are accepted for copying by staff members.[13] The notice must be printed in eighteen-point type, or larger, on heavy paper or other durable material. It must be displayed prominently so that it is clearly visible and comprehensible to a casual observer at the place where orders for staff copying and interlibrary loans are accepted. The notice also must be printed:

... within a box located prominently on the order form itself, either on the front side of the form or immediately adjacent to the space calling for the name or signature of the person [patron] using the

---

NOTICE

Warning Concerning Copyright Restrictions

The copyright law of the United States (Title 17, United States Code) governs the making of photocopies or other reproductions of copyrighted material.

Under certain conditions specified in the law, libraries and archives are authorized to furnish a photocopy or other reproduction. One of these specified conditions is that the photocopy or reproduction is not to be "used for any purpose other than private study, scholarship, or research." If a user makes a request for, or later uses, a photocopy or reproduction for purposes in excess of "fair use," that user may be liable for copyright infringement.

This institution reserves the right to refuse to accept a copying order, if in its judgement, fulfillment of the order would involve violation of copyright law.

Fig. 2. Notice of copyright restrictions

form. The notice shall be printed in type size no smaller than that used predominantly throughout the form, and in no case shall the type size be smaller than 8 points. The notice shall be printed in such a manner as to be clearly legible, comprehensible, and readily apparent to a casual reader of the form.[14]

This part of the regulation applies to order forms patrons use to request photocopies made by a staff member or photocopies obtained through interlibrary loan. It is not necessary for the statement to appear on the interlibrary loan forms sent from one library to another. Some libraries do not ask patrons to submit a written request for staff copying or interlibrary loans. The writer believes that these libraries need not introduce copying request forms merely to comply with this part of the regulation. The notice must only appear on request forms, where such forms are used.

The law also requires that notices appear on or near unsupervised copying machines. This notice is discussed on page 71.

The seventh and eighth requirements forbid copying a large part of a work, multiple copying of a part of a work, and "systematic" copying. They appear in subsection (g):

The rights of reproduction and distribution under this section extend to the isolated and unrelated reproduction or distribution of a single copy or phonorecord of the same material on separate occasions, but do not extend to cases where the library or archives, or its employee—

(1) is aware or has substantial reason to believe that it is engaging in related or concerted reproduction or distribution of multiple copies or phonorecords of the same material, whether made on one occasion or over a period of time, and whether intended for aggregate use by one or more individuals or for separate use by the individual members or a group; or

(2) engages in the systematic reproduction or distribution of single or multiple copies or phonorecords of material described in subsection (d) [Staff-operated copying services]: *Provided,* That nothing in this clause prevents a library or archives from participating in interlibrary arrangements that do not have, as their purpose or effect, that the library or archives receiving such copies or phonorecords for distribution does so in such aggregate quantities as to substitute for a subscription to or purchase of such work.[15]

This section was inserted in the law to prevent abuses of the photocopying exemption. If a library staff member is aware or suspects that a patron is making repeated requests for the same material for the purpose of making multiple copies, the practice must be stopped. Likewise, if a staff member is aware or suspects that a patron is attempting to duplicate an entire work or a large part of it by means of single or repeated requests, this must also be stopped. This section of the law does not appear to cause major problems in handling patrons' requests for copies of books and periodicals in the library's own collection. The greatest impact of this provision falls on interlibrary loan procedures. This controversial problem is discussed in a separate section of the chapter. (See page 73.)

The ninth rule was intended to protect archival materials, but it also applies to libraries. If a library acquires a work under a contractual agreement that prevents the library from copying the work, then the copyright law does not supersede the agreement. These contractual agreements are often found in the fine print in a publisher's catalog and in the fine print on invoices.

The tenth rule states:

The rights of reproduction and distribution under this section do not apply to a musical work, a pictorial, graphic or sculptural work, or a motion picture or other audiovisual work other than an audiovisual work dealing with news, except that no such limitation shall apply with respect to rights granted by subsections (b) [unpublished works] and (c) [duplication of damaged, deteriorating, lost, or stolen works], or with respect to pictorial or graphic works published as illustrations, diagrams, or similar adjuncts to works of which copies are reproduced or distributed in accordance with subsections (d) [copying at a patron's request from the library's own collection] and (e) [copying out-of-print works].[16]

This prevents libraries from copying sheet music, phonograph records, photographic and other pictorial works, sculpture, or audiovisual works, except to replace damaged, lost, stolen, or out-of-print works. These works are known in copyright parlance as performance and display materials. They are treated at length in a later section of this chapter. (See page 80.) Although these materials are closely protected by the law, libraries are permitted to photocopy illustrations when they appear as part of textual materials a patron asks a library to copy.

These ten basic rules apply, with certain variations, to five groups of materials: (1) in-print materials, (2) out-of-print materials, (3) unpublished materials, (4) performance and display materials, and (5) public domain materials.

In-print materials

The reproduction of in-print materials appears to fall into four categories: (1) copying by the staff at the request of a patron, (2) copying by patrons on unsupervised copying machines, (3) copying to replace a lost, damaged, or stolen part of a work, and (4) requesting and making copies for the purpose of interlibrary loans.

Copies made by staff

A library staff member may make a single copy of an article from a periodical or a single copy of a small part of other works for a patron (Rule 4, above) as long as the library complies with the other nine rules.

Unsupervised copier used by patrons

Only one of the basic rules (number 6 on the notice to be placed over machines) applies to unsupervised, patron-operated copiers. The law is precise in identifying the library's responsibilities in regard to these machines:

> Nothing in this section—
>
> (1) shall be construed to impose liability for copyright infringement upon a library or archive or its employees for the unsupervised use of reproducing equipment located on its premises: *Provided,* that such equipment displays a notice that the making of a copy may be subject to the copyright law. . . .[17]

Neither the law nor the reports stipulate the language of this notice; the Copyright Office indicates that it is not responsible for regulating this notice and that it will not do so. The Interlibrary Loan Committee of the American Library Association's Reference and Adult Services Division *recommends* that libraries display the following notice over unsupervised copying machines:

> Notice: The copyright law of the United States (Title 17 U.S. Code) governs the making of photocopies or other reproductions of copyrighted material. The person using this equipment is liable for any infringement.[18]

Some libraries and some photocopying equipment distributors are using notices with different wordings. Any notice of this nature appears to meet the requirement.

The law does not define *unsupervised. Black's Law Dictionary* defines *supervise* as: "To have general oversight over, to superintend or to inspect."[19] Until the courts provide better guidance, it may be safe to assume that a self-service copier located near and in sight of a staff work station is not truly an unsupervised machine. One should not assume from this that all self-service copying machines must be located in an obscure corner, but some prudence should be exercised in placing these machines far enough from a staff work station that the staff member cannot readily see what is being copied. Some smaller libraries use an honor system to collect copying fees from self-service copiers. The patron records or advises the library of the number of copies he or she has made; the fee is then collected from or charged to the patron. In some situations, this may fall within Black's definition of supervision.

One tends to think of self-service machines as coin-operated photocopying machines. Self-service machines also include microform duplicating machines and photographic copystands (i.e., machines that produce photographic prints or slides of graphic and textual materials). These machines must also be considered by a library as it examines its responsibility for managing unsupervised copying machines.

The liability exemption for libraries and library employees in regard to self-service copying machines does not extend to patrons. The law states:

> Nothing in this section—. . .
> (2) excuses a person who uses such [unsupervised] reproducing equipment . . . from liability for copyright infringement for any such act, or for any later use of such copy or phonorecord, if it exceeds fair use as provided by section 107. . . .[20]

Although libraries are not responsible for the unsupervised actions of their patrons, it would behoove libraries to try to educate their patrons about their responsibilities under the copyright law.

Replacement of a lost, damaged, or stolen work

Several basic rules are waived for copying to replace a work that has been lost, damaged, or stolen. The law states:

> The right of reproduction under this section applies to a copy or phonorecord of a published work duplicated in facsimile form solely for the purpose of replacement of a copy or phonorecord that is damaged, deteriorating, lost, or stolen, if the library or archives has, after a reasonable effort, determined that an unused replacement cannot be obtained at a fair price.[21]

This has not been a controversial part of the law, and the House report offers only a brief comment:

> The scope and nature of a reasonable investigation to determine that an unused replacement cannot be obtained will vary according to the circumstances of a particular situation. It will always require recourse to commonly-known trade sources in the United States, and in the normal situation also to the publisher or other copyright owner (if such owner can be located at the address listed in the copyright registration), or an authorized reproducing service.[22]

A work may not be available from the original publisher, but it may be available from a reprint or microform publisher or from a remainder dealer. A library is obligated to check with the original publisher and with these sources before making a copy under the provisions of this section. The greatest problem occurs when libraries attempt to replace a single volume of a multivolume work or a single record in an album. If the work is in print and the publisher cannot replace the missing part or direct the library to an authorized reproduction service, then the library has probably fulfilled the requirements of this section. (Obviously, if a work is in print, it is unlikely that a part will be available from a reprint or microform publisher or from a remainder dealer.) If the work is out of print, then the library must attempt to purchase a copy of the lost, damaged, or missing part from the several sources identified above. If these sources cannot supply "an unused replacement . . . at a fair price," the library is free to reproduce the needed item.[23] The problem occurs when an unused copy of the item is available at a substantial price. Neither the law nor the reports define "fair price." The ALA Resources and Technical Services Division offers the following definition:

1. *Original format*
In order to meet the requirement of fair price, an unused copy of a published copyrighted work should be available at a price as close as possible to the latest suggested retail price.
2. *Reproductions* (photocopy, microform, sound recording copy)
To meet the requirement of fair price, a reproduction of a copyrighted work should be available on a timely basis (within thirty days) at a price which is as close as possible to actual manufacturing costs plus royalty payments.[24]

Interlibrary loan

At the time of writing, interlibrary loan is the most controversial part of the photocopying section of the law. The writer suspects that within a few years, when librarians become accustomed to the requirements, the storm of controversy will pass and interlibrary loan procedures will become relatively routine. The ten basic rules all apply to this service. The law states:

The rights of reproduction and distribution under this section extend to the isolated and unrelated reproduction or distribution of a single copy or phonorecord of the same material on separate occasions, but do not extend to cases where the library or archives, or its employee—
. . .

(2) engages in the systematic reproduction or distribution of single or multiple copies or phonorecords of material described in subsection (d): *Provided,* That nothing in this clause prevents a library or archives from participating in interlibrary arrangements that do not have, as their purpose or effect, that the library or archives receiving such copies or phonorecords for distribution does so in such aggregate quantities as to substitute for a subscription to or purchase of such work.[25]

The House report comments:

This provision . . . provoked a storm of controversy, centering around the extent to which the restrictions on "systematic" activities would prevent the continuation and development of interlibrary networks and other arrangements involving the exchange of photocopies. After thorough consideration, the Committee amended . . . [this section] . . . to add the following proviso:

[The words in the preceding quotation beginning with *Provided.*]
. . .

The key phrases in the Committee's amendment of section 108(g)(2) are "aggregate quantities" and "substitute for a subscription to or purchase of" a work. To be implemented effectively in practice, these provisions will require the development and implementation of more-or-less specific guidelines establishing criteria to govern various situations.[26]

The specific guidelines were developed by the National Commission on the New Technological Uses of Copyrighted Works (CONTU).[27] The text of the guidelines is reproduced in Appendix D. It is a model of opaque legal language, so it may be useful to translate it into common language.

Photocopying from periodicals

1. The record-keeping and copying limitations are based on a calendar year.
2. The guidelines are based on filled or completed interlibrary loan requests. Unfilled requests must be recorded, but they do not apply to the limitations on the number of copies made each year.
3. The restrictions on copying from periodicals apply only to the issues published in the last five years. The guidelines do not restrict the copying of issues that are more than five years old.

4. A statement must be printed, typed, or stamped on the request form indicating that the request complies with section 108(g)(2) of the copyright guidelines. The revised interlibrary loan form of June 29, 1977, includes a check-off box to indicate compliance with this requirement.[28]

5. A library may receive no more than five photocopies per year of articles published in the restricted issue of a periodical. They may be copies of the same article or copies of five different articles.

   For example, a library does not subscribe to *Sunset*. Patrons ask the library to obtain photocopies of certain articles published in the magazine in the last five years, which the library obtains through interlibrary loans. During any calendar year, the library may receive only *five photocopies* of articles published in the magazine in the *last five years*. If the library were to receive a sixth request during that year for an article published in the journal in the last five years, it would face the following alternatives: (1) refuse the request, (2) defer the request to the next calendar year, (3) obtain the photocopy and pay a fee to a periodical clearinghouse (periodical clearinghouses are treated in the following chapter, see page 91), or (4) obtain the permission of the publisher to make the sixth copy.

6. The library placing the requests for the copies maintains records of all requests and the disposition of each request. The records must be retained for three years after the close of the calendar year. (For further information, see Appendix F, "American Library Association Record Maintenance and Retention Guidelines for Interlibrary Loan Departments.")

7. The library supplying the copy must examine each incoming interlibrary loan request for copies to determine if it contains information relative to part 4 above. If the request does not contain information of this nature, it must be rejected.

Photocopying from books. The rules for photocopying parts of books for the purpose of completing interlibrary loan requests are identical to the rules for periodicals, except for item 3. The five-year limitation on copying from periodicals does not apply to books. Libraries are limited to receiving no more than five photocopies per year per title for as long as the copyright on the book is in force. Copyright duration varies from book to book. Under the 1909 law, a book with a valid U.S. copyright was guaranteed twenty-eight years of copyright protection. If the owner renewed the copyright in the twenty-eighth year, and if the copyright was in force on January 1, 1978, the copyright protection lasts seventy-five years. Under the new copyright law, the duration of copyright is the life of the author plus fifty years, or a fixed term of seventy-five years, depending on the form of authorship. (Determining duration of protection is treated in the section on public domain materials, page 82.)

Exceptions. The CONTU guidelines contain two exceptions.

1. If a library owns a copy of a work, but it is prevented for some reason from making photocopies from it, the five copies per year rule is waived. It is not uncommon for a library to own a work that is inaccessible because it has been lost, stolen, damaged, misshelved, and so on. The law and the guidelines are designed to prevent libraries from requesting photocopies of a work to avoid buying or subscribing to the work. The fact that the library owns a copy seemed to be sufficient justification to waive the limitations. This applies "only under those circumstances where the requesting entity would have been able, under the other provisions of section 108, to supply such copy from materials in its own collection."[29] In other words, it does not exempt the library from observing the other regulations in the photocopying section and the CONTU guidelines.

2. The above exemption also applies when the library places an order for the book or periodical. The fact that the material has not arrived is immaterial. Merely placing an order for the work lifts the five-copy limitation, as long as the other parts of the law and the guidelines are observed.

There is no question that the CONTU guidelines are complex and that they add one more burden to the workload of interlibrary loan and network personnel. Existing research on the amount of material copied for interlibrary loan suggests that most libraries rarely place more than five interlibrary loan requests per title per year. Additional studies are underway. One may suspect that they will confirm the earlier research and that most libraries will rarely need to curtail interlibrary loan services to their patrons as a result of the CONTU guidelines. The major problem libraries face is record keeping. Some libraries will want to arrange their completed and pending interlibrary loan request files by title to ascertain that they are not exceeding the five-copy limitation. Other libraries may develop title checklists so each request may be checked off as it is placed. Larger institutions will undoubtedly develop computer-based record-keeping procedures to serve this function.

The CONTU guidelines leave a major question unanswered. The guidelines speak of a "requesting entity."[30] Librarians in state university systems and large school districts wonder if each campus is regarded as a requesting entity or if the entire system must be regarded as the requesting entity. The law and the reports do not answer this question, but there seems to be a consensus that each campus is a separate requesting entity. A variation of that question applies to universities having many libraries. Is each library a requesting entity, or do all of the libraries on campus consist of a single requesting entity? The problem becomes even more complex when some special libraries on a campus are independent units, not administered by the university library system. The writer is not prepared to answer this question, but he suggests that university library administrators act cautiously until better information is available. Continuing studies of the issue should supply a clear answer before long.

The guidelines impose a substantial record-keeping requirement. Libraries are asked to assume an additional, voluntary responsibility. The Register of Copyrights is required to make periodic evaluations of the effect of the photocopying section and the CONTU guidelines. The first report is due January 1, 1983, five years after the law goes into effect. Subsequent reports are due at five-year intervals.[31] The Register would appreciate receiving annual summaries of interlibrary loan transactions from many libraries, both large and small. The Washington Office of the American Library Association is also monitoring this situation and it would also appreciate receiving these annual reports from many libraries.

Out-of-print materials

The ten basic rules, with the exception of rule 4 on the amount of material copied, apply to out-of-print materials. The law states:

The rights of reproduction and distribution under this section apply to the entire work, or to a substantial part of it, made from the collection of a library or archives where the user makes his or her request or from that of another library or archives, if the library or archives has first determined, on the basis of a reasonable investigation, that a copy or phonorecord of the copyrighted work cannot be obtained at a fair price, if—

(1) the copy or phonorecord becomes the property of the user, and the library or archives has had no notice that the copy or phono-record would be used for any purpose other than private study, scholarship, or research; and

(2) the library or archives displays prominently, at the place where orders are accepted, and includes on its order form, a warning of copyright in accordance with requirements that the Register of Copyrights shall prescribe by regulation.[32]

The House committee report states that the investigation of the availability of the work

will always require recourse to commonly-known trade sources in the United States, and in the normal situation also to the publisher or other copyright owner (if the owner can be located at the address listed in the copyright registration), or an authorized reproducing service.[33]

To summarize, before copying all or a substantial part of an out-of-print work, a library must complete the following steps:

1. Ask the publisher in writing if it is actually out of print.
2. If the publisher is not listed in the copyright notice as the copyright owner, also contact the copyright owner to determine that it is indeed out of print.
3. If the publisher or copyright owner advises that the work is out of print, make a reasonable search through bibliographies of works offered in reprint and microform formats to see if it is available from one of these sources.
4. Finally, if it is not available from the above sources, make a reasonable check to see if a copy can be obtained from a remainder or rare book dealer at a fair price. *Fair price* is not defined by the law or reports. *Black's Law Dictionary* states: "The words 'fair price' have been held to be of an ascertainable valuation."[34] It defines valuation as "The act of ascertaining the worth of a thing. The estimated worth of a thing."[35] This seems a bit obscure to those who are not trained in the law. The Implementation of the Copyright Revision Act Committee of the ALA Resources and Technical Services Division suggests that a fair price is "as close

as possible to the latest suggested retail price."[36] This seems to be a reasonable interpretation of the intent of Congress. (The complete text of the document appears in Appendix H.)

In applying this section on the reproduction of out-of-print materials, it is important to keep two exceptions in mind. First, a small part of an out-of-print work (a chapter of a book or an essay from an anthology) may be copied under the simpler guidelines for copying in-print materials discussed earlier on page 70. Secondly, some out-of-print works are in the public domain, in which case they may be copied freely. (Copying public domain materials is treated on page 82.)

Unpublished works

Copyright protection for a work begins the moment it is fixed in a tangible form. Thus, a person's diary or correspondence, an author's manuscript, a student's notes, an artist's sketches, or a filmmaker's storyboard benefit from full and complete copyright protection from the moment they are drawn, written, or recorded. It is not necessary for the creator to add a copyright notice to protect them. They are fully protected, even if the creator is unaware of his or her rights. The creator of the work has the "right of first publication," which permits him or her to determine the time and manner in which the work will be released to the public. As long as the creator does not "publish" the work, he or she may prevent others from copying all or part of it. Unpublished works created after January 1, 1978, are protected for the life of the author, plus fifty years. Copyrights in works created before January 1, 1978, last until December 31, 2002, or under certain circumstances until much later. This careful protection for unpublished materials leads to the common phrase, "there is no fair use copying from unpublished materials." This absolute protection for unpublished works has been slightly breached to permit libraries and archives to duplicate them for the purposes of preservation and security or scholarly research. The law states:

> The rights of reproduction and distribution under this section apply to a copy or phonorecord of an unpublished work duplicated in facsimile form solely for purposes of preservation and security or for deposit for research use in another library or archives of the type described by clause (2) of subsection (a) [open to the public or open

to researchers], if the copy or phonorecord reproduced is currently in the collections of the library or archives.[37]

The House report adds:

> Under this exemption, for example, a repository could make photocopies of manuscripts by microfilm or electrostatic process, but could not reproduce the work in "machine-readable" language for storage in an information system.[38]

There are two important points here. First, the copy can only be made by the library or archive owning the original copy. (It is a reasonable assumption that if the original were lost or destroyed, a library owning a copy could make another copy under the terms of this section of the law.) Second, the copy must be retained by the library holding the original or deposited in an approved library. The copy may not be given or sold to an individual, but the individual may borrow it from the library or archive.

The section generally speaks of duplicating unpublished textual materials and sound recordings. Section 108(h) makes it clear that it also applies to duplicating unpublished photographs, motion picture films, and so on, for the purpose of preservation or scholarship. Additional guidance on this problem is found in the fair use section of the law. (See "Preservation of Out-of-Print Materials" on page 46.)

In 2003, many unpublished materials will enter the public domain permitting individuals and institutions to reproduce them freely. (See "Public Domain Materials" on page 82.)

Performance and display materials

Performance and display materials are carefully protected from unauthorized copying. Performance materials are those designed to be recited, rendered, played, danced, or acted,

> either directly or by means of any device or process or, in the case of a motion picture or other audiovisual work, to show its images in any sequence or to make the sounds accompanying it audible.[39]

Display materials are items designed for public display. They include paintings, prints, photographs, photographic slides, individual frames of motion picture films, tapestries, and pottery.

This section will only treat the copying of these materials. (Performances and displays are discussed on pages 34 and 57.) The law states:

> The rights of reproduction and distribution under this section
> [Section 108] do not apply to a musical work, a pictorial, graphic
> or sculptural work, or a motion picture or other audiovisual
> work. . . .[40]

The law is quite precise about forbidding the copying of the above-mentioned items. The law and the reports also provide exceptions. (1) Unpublished materials may be duplicated for the purpose of preservation or security or to make them available to another library or archive for the purpose of scholarship. This exemption was treated in the preceding section. (See page 79.) (2) Libraries may duplicate pictures, graphs, charts, and other illustrations found among textual materials in books and periodicals copied in the process of duplicating the textual materials. (3) Libraries may reproduce small parts of these works for scholarly purposes. The House report comments:

> Although subsection (h) generally removes musical, graphic, and
> audiovisual works from the specific exemptions of section 108, it
> is important to recognize that the doctrine of fair use under
> section 107 remains fully applicable to the photocopying or other
> reproduction of such works. In the case of music, for example, it
> would be fair use for a scholar doing musicological research to have
> a library supply a copy of a portion of a score or to reproduce
> portions of a phonorecord of a work. Nothing in section 108 impairs
> the applicability of the fair use doctrine to a wide variety of situations
> involving photocopying or other reproduction by a library of
> copyrighted material in its collection, where the user requests the
> reproduction for legitimate scholarly or research purposes.[41]

This creates another of those gray areas that require good judgment. The statement does not give a library the right to copy an entire score or an entire record; it only suggests that copying a small part of the work for scholarly purposes is acceptable. This repeats the basic theme in the preceding chapter on fair use; it is a fair use of a copyrighted material to copy a small part of the work for the purpose of scholarship, criticism, or teaching. (The relationship between section 107 on fair use and section 108 on library photocopying is discussed on page 85.)

The fourth exemption affects audiovisual news programs. "Audiovisual news programs" is a legal phrase meaning television news programs. A last-minute amendment to the Copyright Law enabled libraries and archives to videotape these programs. This was a direct outgrowth of the Columbia Broadcasting System (CBS) suit against Vanderbilt University. The university operates a television news archive that videotapes regularly scheduled television news programs. It makes copies of the programs and edits them for the convenience of researchers. CBS sued the university for an infringement of their copyrights in the programs. The matter was effectively resolved when Congress accepted Senator Howard Baker's amendment permitting libraries and archives to videotape these news programs. CBS dropped its suit against the university, and the university dropped its countersuit against CBS. The matter seems to be resolved, at least to the satisfaction of libraries and archives. The Conference Committee report comments on this exemption:

> The conference committee is aware that an issue has arisen as to the meaning of the phrase "audiovisual news program" in section 108(f)(3). The conferees believe that, under the provision as adopted in the conference substitute, a library or archives qualifying under section 108(a) [not-for-profit requirement] would be free, without regard to the archival activities of the Library of Congress or any other organization, to reproduce, on videotape or any other medium of fixation or reproduction, local, regional, or network newscasts, interviews concerning current news events, and on-the-spot coverage of news events, and to distribute a limited number of reproductions of such a program on a loan basis.[42]

These regularly scheduled newscasts would include the daily news programs as well as the regularly scheduled weekend news programs. The interviews concerning current news events can be found in regularly scheduled news programs, in interview format programs, and in other programming. (Additional information about videotaping television programs off-air is found in the preceding chapter under "Off-Air Copying of Television Programs," page 41.)

Public domain materials

A published work that is not protected by a valid copyright is in the public domain. If a work is in the public domain, no one may claim ownership of the expressions contained in the work. A work enters the public domain in any one of three ways: (1) publication without a proper notice (publication without notice is treated in the section on omission or removal of the entire copyright notice, page 112), (2) termination of the copyright at the end of the period of protection, and (3) failure to renew copyrights in the twenty-eighth year in works created before January 1, 1978. Once a work has entered the public domain, it is not eligible for copyright protection, and it may be copied freely.

Although a work may be in the public domain, later derivative works (works based on the original) may still be protected. The 1858 edition of *Gray's Anatomy* is in the public domain, but later editions are still protected by valid copyrights. Scholarly reprints of works in the public domain frequently appear with a copyright notice. This notice protects only the newly created introductions, commentaries, notes, and so on.

If a work published before January 1, 1978, does not have a copyright notice, it is probably in the public domain. A number of scholarly and professional associations deliberately publish their pamphlets and journals without a copyright notice, so they may be copied freely. U.S. government publications are published without a copyright notice; they are in the public domain. Government publications occasionally contain copyrighted materials, and these materials must be given the respect due to a copyrighted work. Occasionally, a work is accidentally published without a copyright notice. The new law has provisions permitting the copyright owner to take steps to retain the copyright. Unless one is aware that the work is protected, it is safe to assume that the work is in the public domain.[43]

A work that has a copyright notice may be in the public domain. Works copyrighted before January 1, 1978, that were renewed in the twenty-eighth year and were protected by a valid copyright on January 1, 1978, now have seventy-five years of copyright protection. Thus, a work is in the public domain if it was copyrighted before January 1, 1978, and is more than seventy-five years old. (The exception is discussed later.)

Because of changes in the copyright law affecting the duration of copyright protection, all works copyrighted in the United States before September 19, 1906, are in the public domain. (The exception is discussed later.)

Occasionally a work will have several dates in the copyright notice. A notice might read: Copyright, 1900, 1910, 1931, XYZ Publishing Co. The first edition was published in 1900. It was revised or updated in 1910 and 1931. The material published in 1900 is in the public domain. The material added in the 1910 revision will probably go into the public domain in 1985; the material added in 1931 will probably go into the public domain in 2006. Unless the original work and the revisions are clearly distinguishable, treat it as a validly copyrighted work.

The 1909 copyright law, and its predecessor the 1870 law, required that the copyright be renewed in its twenty-eighth year if it was to receive the full term of protection. If the copyright was not renewed in the twenty-eighth year, the work entered the public domain at the end of the twenty-eighth year. Many works were not renewed, and they have entered the public domain. Most commercial publishing firms are careful to preserve the copyrights in their works. Some publishers and professional associations are careless about this matter. Many early twentieth-century films entered the public domain because the copyright proprietors failed to renew the copyrights. Some works entered the public domain because the ownership of the rights was unclear. The new copyright law did not remove the requirement to renew. Works created before January 1, 1978, must be renewed during the twenty-eighth year to receive the full seventy-five years of protection.

It is relatively easy to determine that a work has entered the public domain. Registrations and renewals are published in the *Catalog of Copyright Entries,* which is available in many college and university libraries and in some large public libraries.[44] If a renewal entry does not appear in the catalog, the work is probably in the public domain. The Copyright Office will conduct this search for ten dollars per hour. One may also conduct a personal search at the Copyright Office in Arlington, Virginia. A Copyright Office pamphlet, "How to Investigate the Copyright Status of a Work," provides further information about the search process.[45] It is available without charge from the Copyright Office.

A special extension of copyright duration was granted for Mary Baker Eddy's *Science and Health with Key to the Scriptures.* The copyright in this work, and in variant titles of the work, extends for seventy-five years from the effective date of the act (December 15, 1971) or from the date of first publication, whichever is later.[46]

Works created after January 1, 1978, enter the public domain fifty years after the death of the author or the last surviving coauthor. The earliest date one of these works could enter the public domain is December 31, 2028.

Foreign copyrights are protected in the United States by a number of international agreements. The duration of foreign copyrights can be complicated. Many industrial nations provide a copyright duration of the life of the author plus fifty years. At least one country provides a duration of the life of the author plus seventy-five years. Some works may have been given an extended duration, similar to the one given to Mary Baker Eddy's *Science and Health with Key to the Scriptures.* It would be advisable to seek the advice of a competent copyright attorney before assuming that a foreign work copyrighted in the last two hundred years is in the public domain.

Photocopying and fair use

It was noted in the preceding chapter that the fair use and photocopying sections of the new copyright law originated in the judicial concept of fair use. This was the basis of the government's defense of the National Library of Medicine in the Williams & Wilkins case. This judicial concept that one may copy or otherwise use a small portion of a copyrighted work for the purpose of criticism, comment, scholarship, research, or teaching is the basis of both the photocopying and fair use sections of the law. The congressional reports generally speak of fair use as it applies to teachers. The law and the reports are clear, though, that fair use has broader applications. The Senate report on the fair use section contains references to libraries, including one reference to public libraries. The importance of the fair use section to libraries is reinforced by a statement in the photocopying section: "Nothing in this section— . . . in any way affects the right of fair use as provided by section 107. . . ."[47] Section 108(f)(2) comments that copying by patrons on self-service copying machines must meet the fair use criteria. One may then ask, what rights does the fair use section give to libraries that are not provided in the photocopying section? There are undoubtedly many rights, but one right is especially obvious. The photocopying section, with one exception, limits copying to single copies. That exception deals with television news programs. The fair use section permits an individual or institution to make multiple copies of small parts of a work for class distribution. The restrictions on making multiple copies center on (1) the use of the copies, (2) the type of materials copied, (3) the number of copies made, and (4) the effect of the copying on the market for the work. There is no hint or suggestion that the copies cannot be made in libraries by library employees. In many instances, libraries are the logical (or only) place for teachers to obtain multiple photocopies of materials for class distribution. A library cannot justify refusing to make multiple copies for class use on the basis of the single-copy limitation in the photocopying section of the law. This application of the fair use section usually applies to school, college, and university libraries; it also applies to public and special libraries used by teachers.

One common application of fair use in libraries involves making multiple copies of articles to be placed on reserve for class use. Many teachers and educational administrators are concerned about the expenditure of scarce funds and scarce natural resources required to make multiple copies of materials for class distribution. Many institutions have developed a compromise measure to reduce the number of items they must reproduce for student use. They only make one copy of an article for every eight or ten or fifteen students in the class, and the copies are placed on reserve in the library. Librarians who are attuned to the single-copy requirements of the photocopying section are sometimes reluctant to accept this practice. It is clearly at odds with the single-copy regulations in the photocopying section. But, when conducted within the requirements of the fair use section, it seems to fall within the intended limits of that section. The congressional reports on the fair use section suggest limits to the number of items a teacher may copy (or have copied) for class distribution during each term. As long as the reproduction of multiple copies for class distribution *and* the alternative of placing multiple copies on reserve fall within these guidelines, it is probably a fair use. Naturally, the other requirements of the fair use section must also be met.[48]

The congressional reports take a liberal position on fair use copying of newspapers and news magazines. It might be acceptable for a library to make multiple copies of news materials on demand from a patron. It would not be advisable to use this provision to copy newspapers or magazines currently available at newsstands. The provision is more appropriately used to make copies from issues that are no longer available from publishers or vendors.

In some instances, the fair use section permits libraries to copy materials that cannot be copied under the terms of the photocopying section. Section 108(h) prohibits libraries from copying sheet music. The "[Fair Use] Guidelines for Educational Uses of Music" permits emergency copying of sheet music.[49] If the emergency copying meets the fair use guidelines, then a library would be justified in making the copy, even though it *appears* to violate the requirements in section 108(h). Other examples will undoubtedly be found as the profession gains experience with the law.

Obtaining permission

Librarians, teachers, and educational specialists frequently need to duplicate or adapt all or a large part of a copyrighted work. This frequently exceeds the limits of the fair use or photocopying sections of the law. If it does, one is obligated to obtain permission to duplicate or adapt the material. There are a number of procedures used to grant permission or to transfer rights in a work. They are (1) transfer of ownership, (2) compulsory licenses, (3) voluntary licenses, (4) clearinghouses, (5) one-time permissions, and (6) purchase conditions.

Transfer of ownership

Ownership of a copyright is transferred by several devices. It may be bequeathed by will or pass as personal property when the owner dies without a will. The entire copyright, or a portion of it (e.g., movie rights), may be sold. The ownership is transferred by means of a contract; the contract may and probably should be registered at the Copyright Office. This form of transfer is not often used by schools and libraries, but it is commonly used in the publishing and entertainment industries.

Compulsory licenses

Compulsory licenses were introduced in the 1909 copyright law. Manufacturers of "mechanical reproductions" of musical compositions such as phonograph records were required to pay the composer a royalty of two cents for each "part" manufactured.[1] A record having one song on each side contained two parts; thus, four cents from the sale of the record went to the composer. The manufacturer could only reproduce compositions previously recorded with the composer's consent. The 1976 copyright law increases the royalty rate to "either two and three-fourth cents, or one-half of one cent per minute of playing time or fraction thereof, whichever amount is larger."[2]

The new copyright law established compulsory licenses for jukeboxes, cable television, and nonprofit radio and television stations. Jukeboxes were quite new when the 1909 law was passed. Congress was unable to arrive at a suitable royalty payment structure for the music played on the machines, so they were exempted from royalty payments. The omission was corrected in the new copyright law. The owners must register the machines with the Copyright Office and pay an eight dollar per year fee for each machine. The income is divided among the copyright owners of the music performed on the machines, based on a performance sampling system.

Commercial cable television (CATV) operators must pay royalties for the "distant" television signals they transmit through their systems. They do not pay royalties for the local stations and the instructional broadcasts they carry. The royalty rates are established through a complicated sliding scale based on gross receipts from subscribers to the CATV system and the number of distant signals transmitted. Hotel and apartment cable systems, instructional cable systems, government and nonprofit cable systems, and passive carriers such as translators are exempt from making the payments.

Nonprofit broadcast stations, including instructional radio and television stations, are required to pay royalties for the transmission of "published nondramatic musical works and published pictorial, graphic and sculptural works. . . ."[3] Congress asked the broadcasters and the copyright owners to arrive at a royalty payment schedule for these works through a voluntary agreement. If they failed to reach agreement, the law specified that the rates were to be set by the Copyright Royalty Tribunal.

The tribunal is a five-member body created by the new copyright law to resolve a number of royalty problems generated by the new law. The copyright owners and the broadcasters were unable to arrive at an agreement, and at the time of this writing, the tribunal had not had time to conduct the hearings and to set the rates.

Voluntary licenses

Voluntary licenses are widely used and come in a variety of forms. They are essentially contracts, conferring part of the copyright owner's bundle of rights on the licensee. Licenses may be exclusive or nonexclusive; this permits the copyright owner to sell similar or identical licenses to other institutions. Licenses permitting schools and libraries to videotape educational films are readily available. Making videotape copies of films extends the life of the film and permits the school to make enough copies to satisfy all requests for the title. When the title is no longer needed, it can be erased and a different film can be recorded on the tape. Almost all educational film distributors now offer these licenses. The terms of these licenses vary from company to company, and they are often negotiable.

Program duplication licenses are also sold by the commercial television networks. They permit the buyer to videotape regularly scheduled news programs off the air for delayed use in a school or library. The provisions in section 108(f)(3) of the new law seem to make these licenses unnecessary for school or library use. The networks do not accept that interpretation, and the question may have to be settled in the courts.

Radio and television stations obtain the right to broadcast films and other prerecorded programs through voluntary contracts. These are frequently sold as exclusive licenses, so the copyright owner cannot sell the program to other stations in the licensing or viewing area.

Blanket licenses are available for the duplication of background music, short musical segments, and sound effects used in producing radio, television, and audiovisual programs. These licenses are described under "Cleared Music" on pages 99-102.

Clearinghouses

A clearinghouse is a central agency that grants permission to duplicate copyrighted materials owned by the participants in the clearinghouse. The clearinghouse collects royalty payments for copies and disburses the receipts to the copyright owners. In some instances, permission to copy is granted automatically through compulsory licenses or by an open permission to make the copies. The American Society of Composers, Authors and Publishers (ASCAP) is a performing rights society which is, in essence, a clearinghouse for royalty payments for the performing rights (or small rights) in musical compositions. Radio and television stations and the networks acquire voluntary licenses from ASCAP for the music used in their programs. Movie producers and wired-music services such as Muzak also obtain licenses from the society. ASCAP provides other services for their members, including performance sampling, educational services, and legal services, but it is essentially a very efficient clearinghouse for a large body of musical copyrights. Smaller musical clearinghouses are operated by Broadcast Music Inc. (BMI) and SESAC (formerly the Society of European Stage Authors and Composers).

A journal article clearinghouse was established in 1977 by the Association of American Publishers (AAP). The AAP Copyright Clearance Center (CCC) began operations on January 1, 1978, the day the new copyright law went into effect.[4] It concentrates on technical, scientific, and medical journals, but it also serves other journal publications. CCC accepts payments for the duplication of journal articles when the number of copies exceeds the fair use and photocopying limitations. The center also accepts payments for *types* of copying that are outside the bounds of the law. Some special libraries examine incoming journals and make single and multiple copies of relevant articles for distribution to the scientists served by the library. This is contrary to the single-copy-on-demand concept in the library photocopying section. Under most circumstances it also exceeds the limitations of the fair use section, especially the fourth criterion. (The fourth criterion speaks to the impact of copying on the market for or value of the work being copied.)

Publishers participating in CCC place a notice on the first page of each article. The notice identifies the copying fee for the article and the identification code for the article and the journal. The antitrust laws prevent publishers from establishing uniform copying fees. Some publishers require a uniform copying fee for all articles, while other publishers have a range of fees based on the length or importance of the articles.

Obtaining permission

The center offers a number of participation procedures for libraries and copying centers. They all require the library or copying center to submit a statement of its intention to participate in the service. Each participant is assigned an account number. One proposed payment procedure would enable the participant to obtain a metering device, similar to a postage meter. A metered stamp for the value of the article would be attached to each copy. Fair use copies would receive a stamp for $00.00. Another system requires a participant to open a deposit account with the center. The participant maintains a record of the charges and sends a monthly statement applying the charges against the deposit. The simplest procedure, and the one best suited to most libraries, requires the library to make an extra copy of the first page of each article made *in excess* of the fair use or photocopying requirements. The payment and the extra copies of the title pages are sent to the center once a month. This may be an excellent solution for libraries that make more interlibrary loan requests than the CONTU guidelines permit. It may also be useful for libraries that make multiple copies of articles, in excess of the multiple copying limits of the fair use section of the law. Some publishers will not be participating in this clearinghouse. Libraries and copying centers will have to obtain permission directly from these publishers.

There has been some discussion in recent years of establishing a clearinghouse for audiovisual materials. Such an event does not appear to be in the offing, though. An effective clearinghouse may be difficult to establish since many producers do not have full rights to the materials they sell. They frequently obtain a one-time permission to incorporate the visual or aural materials in their programs. This prevents them from giving others permission to make copies. One major producer, Encyclopaedia Britannica Educational Corporation, offers an index to the scenes in the firm's 16mm films. They will supply a 16mm film copy of the scenes a producer wishes to incorporate in a new film or video program.

One-time permissions

One-time or single-use permissions are widely used by publishers to obtain permission to reprint poems, essays, and long quotations in their books. Audiovisual producers often obtain one-time permissions to incorporate pictures, film clips, and other items in their programs. Educational institutions use this procedure to obtain permission to make copies of a work or to adapt a work to another form. The permission applies to a single application of copying, editing, etc. Teachers have recently begun using this procedure to obtain permission to duplicate materials for class distribution. The fair use section of the committee reports indicates that teachers have limited rights to make multiple copies of articles, essays, poems, and the like for class distribution. However, this right can only be used for a limited number of times each term. In addition, this right only applies to copying a small part of a work. If the amount of material or the number of copies exceeds the limits, the teacher must obtain permission for this action. Libraries are generally limited to making single copies of parts of copyrighted works for their patrons or for internal use. (The exceptions are treated in the section on "The Relationship Between the Photocopying and Fair Use Sections of the Law" on page 85.) A library that wants to make multiple copies of an item for staff training or for patron use can use the one-time permission procedure to obtain permission.

Obtaining one-time or single-use permission is quite simple. One writes to the publisher or producer and asks for permission to make the copies. The request identifies the materials to be copied, the number and type of copies to be made, and the manner in which the copies are to be used. Most publishers and producers respond within three weeks, and they are usually generous in giving educational institutions permission to make the copies without charge. Some publishers and producers charge a small copying fee, but the fees are usually quite modest. There are two problems with this procedure. First, many applicants fail to supply all of the necessary information with their requests. Second, a small minority of publishers and producers do not respond to these requests. The first problem can be overcome by using a suitable application form, such as the request form in figure 3. It is based on information obtained from publications of the Association of American Publishers, the Association of Media Producers, and a recent dissertation.[5] Readers who use the form correctly and who observe the following points should experience little difficulty in obtaining permission.

Permissions Dept.   Name of institution
Publisher/Producer   Mailing address
Address   Date

Gentlepersons,

Please may I have permission to duplicate the following for the
purpose of: _____
Title: _____
Copyright owner: _____
Author: _____
Pages/frames: _____
Number of copies: _____
Type of reproduction: _____
Distributed to: _____
The copies will be distributed free of charge for single use by the
above.

Sincerely,

Printed name
Title

Fig. 3. Request form

Recommendations for use

1. Use a standard request form, such as the one in figure 3 or a
   form provided by a trade association.
2. Identify the institution where the copies will be used. This
   can be accomplished by reproducing the form on the institution's letterhead.
3. Identify the person making the request.
4. *Fully* identify the work to be copied.
5. Identify the parts to be copied or omitted from the copies.
6. When asking permission to copy parts of a book, send a
   photocopy of the parts to be copied. This shortens the publisher's searching time.
7. Identify the persons who will use the copies (e.g., the English
   101 class).
8. Advise, when appropriate, that the copies will be distributed
   free of charge.

9. Advise, when appropriate, that the copies will only be used one time.
10. Leave a four-inch margin at the bottom of the form for the publisher's or producer's response. Many publishers and producers use a rubber stamp or a handwritten note on the bottom of the form to grant permission.
11. Allow four weeks for a reply.
12. Send a stamped, addressed return envelope. Many publishers and producers discard it and use their own envelope and postage. Some publishers and producers may not reply if a stamped, addressed return envelope is not provided. Let experience dictate the application of this point.[6]

Out-of-print sheet music

The Music Library Association (MLA), the Music Publishers' Association (MPA), and the National Music Publishers' Association (NMPA) have a standard application form for one-time permission to duplicate out-of-print sheet music. It is shown as figure 4; readers are urged to use this form to obtain permission to duplicate sheet music. One requirement for this procedure is at variance from the above list of recommendations. The requesting library must send *two* copies of each request. The publisher will retain one copy. The other copy is returned to the requesting library with a notation granting or denying permission to copy.

Dealing with nonresponders

The publishers' and producers' trade associations have tried to persuade publishers and producers to be responsive to requests for permission from schools and libraries. The great majority of these firms handle this service promptly and courteously. There are a few firms, however, that will not respond to requests. Frustrated educators have suggested an alternate tactic for dealing with these firms, which employs a letter or form advising that the copies will be made unless the firm forbids the copying within a specified time. Thirty days is the most commonly suggested time span. This is sometimes called a notification permission form. Its legality is open to question. It is a unilateral contract by nonresponse. The recipient of the contract (the form) is understood to agree to the terms of the contract

To _____ Date _____
       (name of publisher)

We require the work(s) entitled:

_____

_____

1. If in print, please send us _____ copies of the work(s) and bill us.

2. If permanently out of print, please sign the duplicate of this form, which shall constitute permission by you to use to make or procure the making of _____ copies of the work(s) for delivery to:

_____

_____

subject to the following conditions:

    a. The copyright notice shall appear on all copies.

    b. No recording use or performance for profit use or use other than library use shall be made of any copy unless such use shall be expressly licensed by you or an agent or organization acting on your behalf.

    c. We shall pay _____ for the right to copy pursuant to this permission but not otherwise.

3. If any work referred to above is not in your catalog, please insert an X here _____ and return the duplicate of this form to us promptly.

AGREED TO: Very truly yours,

_____   _____
  (name of publisher)   (name of library)

By _____   By _____

This form should be prepared in duplicate.

Fig. 4. Permission to copy out-of-print sheet music

by not responding. The firm must take action if the terms are not acceptable. This is somewhat at odds with the traditional contract agreement in which both parties indicate their acceptance of the terms by signing a document. It is also at odds with the newer unilateral contract by fulfillment. In this instance, one party proposes terms and the second party accepts the terms by acting on them. (For example, a person calls a fuel oil dealer and asks the dealer to sell and to deliver one hundred gallons of fuel oil at the prevailing price. The dealer indicates an acceptance of the terms by delivering the oil.)

Publishers' and producers' responses to the notification permission form were tested in a recent dissertation.[7] The study demonstrated that many publishers and producers who ignore conventional request forms, such as the one in figure 3, also ignore the notification permission form. One assumes that they received the form and acquiesced to its terms (an unwise assumption, considering the inadequacies of the U.S. postal system). A few publishers and producers who ignored the conventional request form responded to the notification permission form by granting permission to make the copies. Other publishers and producers who ignored the conventional request form responded to the notification form by denying permission to make copies. The major question about this procedure is not whether it works, but whether it is legal. There are conflicting answers to this question. An attorney for a major book and audiovisual firm publicly recommends that it be used. Equally competent attorneys question its legality. A law school professor who specializes in copyright commented that the legality of the procedure is open to question, but if he were a school district attorney he would recommend using it when necessary. A permissions officer for a publishing firm indicated that the firm uses this procedure for obtaining permission from foreign copyright owners. The author is not prepared to offer legal advice on this point. He would suggest, however, that schools and libraries should not use the procedure without the approval of the institution's attorney. Schools and libraries that use the form should consider the following points:

1. Limit its use to publishers and producers who do not respond to more conventional procedures. The research seems

to suggest that publishers and producers who are responsive to conventional requests are less receptive to this procedure.[8]

2. Retain copies of all correspondence pertaining to the request.
3. Send the form by certified mail with a return receipt. This proves that the publisher or producer received your correspondence. It does not prove that the correspondence contained a notification permission form.

A copy of a notification permission form is shown in figure 5.

Permissions Dept.   Name of institution
Publisher/Producer   Mailing address
Address   Date

Gentlepersons,

We know that you are busy and that it is time consuming to reply to requests for permission to copy small parts of your publications or productions. It may be simpler for all of us if we inform you that we plan to duplicate portions of the item identified below for use in this institution. If we do not receive a message from you within thirty days from the above date, we will assume that you have agreed to grant permission to duplicate this copyrighted material.

Title: _____

Copyright owner: _____

Author: _____

Pages/frames: _____

Number of copies: _____

Type of reproduction: _____

Distributed to: _____

Used for: _____

The copies will be distributed free of charge for single use by the above.

                              Sincerely,

                              Printed name
                              Title

Fig. 5. Notification form

Prepaid permission

Persons who are uncomfortable with the above procedure have suggested an alternative. If a publisher or producer will not respond to a conventional request for permission, then send a check for one dollar along with a form requesting and paying for the permission. Presumably, if the check is cashed, the publisher or producer agrees to the request. There is some logic to this proposal. Many of the publishers and producers who do not respond to more conventional requests are small firms. The owner may not understand the importance some clients attach to a permissions service. An unanticipated check in the mail, even a check for one dollar, may be an effective way to gain their attention and to achieve permission. If the check is marked "void after thirty days from the date issued," it may accelerate the response. Permission is presumably granted when the check is cashed or deposited. A library or school that has not been able to obtain permission through the normal procedures may wish to consider this approach. The author is not aware that this procedure has been used, and it would be well to clear it with the institution's attorney before employing it. A sample prepaid permission form is shown in figure 6.

Cleared music

The producers of audiovisual programs frequently incorporate music in their programs. These musical selections include background music for the title and credit frames, mood music for nonnarrated scenes, musical bridges between scenes, and musical stings for dramatic effect. An infrequent use of a very small part of a copyrighted recording may be a fair use if the use conforms to the fair use requirements. Producers often use several musical segments in their programs, and they anticipate a long-term use and a widespread distribution of their programs. This seems to preclude a fair use of the musical segments. Some producers have attempted to obtain permission to incorporate popular music in their programs. They usually find that it is either prohibitively expensive or impossible to obtain this permission. The difficulty in obtaining permission results from the dual copyright protection given to music. The original musical composition (the sheet music) is protected by one copyright and the performance is protected by a second copyright. To repro-

Permissions Dept.   Name of institution
Publisher/Producer   Mailing address
Address   Date

Gentlepersons,

Attached is a check for one dollar ($1) in payment for duplicating the copyrighted materials identified below. Cashing this check or depositing it in a bank will signify your acceptance of this agreement.

Title: _____

Copyright owner: _____

Author: _____

Pages/frames: _____

Number of copies: _____

Type of reproduction: _____

Distributed to: _____

Used for: _____

The copies will be distributed free of charge for single use by the above.

Sincerely,

Printed name
Title

Fig. 6. Prepaid permission

duce one of these recordings, one must obtain the permission of both copyright owners. The procedure is further complicated by the contractual agreements between the producers and the musicians' unions. Audiovisual producers find that the only reliable way to obtain music for their productions is to use cleared music. Cleared music is recorded under contractual agreements which permit the producer to sell recording rights for the performances.

To use cleared music, a producer purchases recordings from a cleared music firm. Most firms offer substantial libraries of short musical selections designed for use in audiovisual programs. The producer incorporates the music in a program and pays the cleared music firm for its use. The payment permits the producer to make unlimited numbers of copies of the program. The only substantial restriction on the use of this music concerns radio and television broadcasts. If the program is to be broadcast, the producer frequently must pay a broadcast fee to the cleared music firm.

There are three basic procedures for paying for cleared music: (1) a per-use fee, usually called a needle-drop fee, (2) a per-program fee, and (3) an annual license. (One West Coast cleared music firm offers a one-time payment plan; after purchasing the recordings from the firm—at a substantial price—the purchaser may incorporate the music in any number of programs without further payment of needle-drop or blanket fees. This could be advantageous to institutions that do not require a large cleared music library.)

Needle-drop fees. Per-use fees vary from one firm to another, but they are often twenty to twenty-five dollars per use. A producer pays a needle-drop fee for each segment of music incorporated in a program. If the fee is twenty dollars and a program contains two musical segments, then the producer pays forty dollars for the use of the music. The producer is then free to reproduce and distribute the program within the limits of the agreement. These fees appear to be negotiable.

Per-program fees. Producers may pay a single fee for all of the music in a program. These are known as per-film or per-production blanket fees. They are especially useful for programs containing numerous musical segments. The fee is based on the running time of the program; it is also based on whether the music is used in a nonprofit or for-profit venture and the type of distribution planned. A typical rate card reads:

Up to 15 minutes	$ 75
Up to 30 minutes	100
Up to 45 minutes	125
Up to 60 minutes	150

These fees appear to be negotiable.

Annual licenses. An annual license or annual blanket license permits a production center to make unlimited use of the music covered by the license. The rates for an annual license vary substantially according to the size of the production operation and the use of the programs produced in the center. The rates are negotiable and commonly start at $500 per year. The writer knows of one small commercial production firm that paid $250 for an annual blanket license. The firm produces instructional audiocassettes containing short musical segments at the beginning and end of each tape.

Most cleared music firms are found in New York and Los Angeles. They may be identified in the *Audiovisual Market Place: A Multimedia Guide* under the heading "Music & Sound Effects Libraries."[9] Some of these firms also offer sound effects recordings for reproduction under similar agreements.

Purchase conditions

Purchase conditions are widely used by institutional purchasing agents to insure that the materials and services purchased by the institution are safe, effective, delivered on time, and installed correctly. The supplier accepts the terms when he or she accepts the order. Suppliers use somewhat similar conditions-of-sale requirements, which appear in sales brochures, catalogs, order forms, and invoices. Purchase order requirements and sales condition requirements are contractual agreements between the purchaser and seller.

A buyer is free to include a requirement in a purchase order stipulating that the copyrighted materials purchased through the order may be duplicated. A purchase condition might read: Purchase contingent on the right to make two additional copies of each title. If the publisher or producer does not wish to accept these terms, he or she must refuse the order or renegotiate the terms. It is important that these purchase conditions be printed or typed on all copies of the order form. It is not sufficient to list the conditions on an attached form. If questions were raised at a later date about the duplication of copyrighted materials, the purchaser must be able to demonstrate that the purchase order contained such a requirement. It might be difficult to prove that an attachment appeared on the vendor's copy.

The following are examples of purchase conditions:

Purchase contingent on the right to—
> make a circulating copy for use by the patrons of XYZ Library.
> make three copies for use by students in XYZ School.
> transfer the program to a four-track format for use in a dial access system at XYZ College.
> transfer the program to a videocassette format for use by students at XYZ School.

If a vendor rejects the order because of the terms, the buyer must reorder the item without the conditions or forego purchasing the item. Very few firms reject orders because of these terms.[10]

There are two important limitations on the use of purchase conditions. First, the owner of the particular rights in the works is the only one able to grant permission to duplicate the material. The national distributor is often the owner of these rights. Purchase orders containing this permission clause must be sent to this party.

Second, these conditions should not be used to purchase musical recordings. The dual copyright protection for musical recordings (dual protection was treated in the "Cleared Music" section on page 99) makes it virtually impossible for the producers of musical recordings to accede to these requirements. These purchase specifications should be limited to spoken word recordings and to audiovisual programs that are essentially non-musical in nature.

Purchase conditions stipulating the right to duplicate copyrighted materials are not commonly used, and vendors do not expect to find them on orders. Both contractual and ethical considerations require that the purchaser draw the vendor's attention to these special requirements.[11] A note attached to the purchase order should suffice. Schools and libraries should not use this procedure without the approval of the institution's attorney.

Securing
copyright protection

The Copyright Revision Act of 1976 provides automatic copyright protection for a work the moment it is written, recorded, or otherwise fixed in a tangible form. The creator receives this protection without being aware that the work is protected. This protection may be lost, though, when the work is published. A copyright notice must appear on all published copies to preserve the copyright protection in the work. The law defines publication as

> the distribution of copies or phonorecords of a work to the public by sale or other transfer of ownership, or by rental, lease, or lending. The offering to distribute copies or phonorecords to a group of persons for purpose of further distribution, public performance, or public display, constitutes publication.[1]

An instructor's bibliography or course outline receives full copyright protection the moment it is written. The copyright may be lost when copies are distributed to a class, unless a proper copyright notice is placed on all copies. Two additional steps may be taken to protect the author's rights in the work: (1) registering the work with the Copyright Office, and (2) depositing copies of the work at the Copyright Office. Under the 1909 copyright law, two of these steps (placing a correct notice in the work and depositing copies) were taken to *obtain* federal copyright protection; under the 1976 law only the first step (inserting the notice) must be taken to *retain* federal copyright protection in the work.

The notice

A copyright notice consists of three parts: (1) the word *Copyright,* or the abbreviation *Copr.,* or the © symbol; (2) the name of the copyright owner; and (3) the year of first publication. This notice must appear in all copies sold or otherwise distributed to the public. (Special requirements for notices on sound recordings and certain other materials are treated in the "Special Copyright Notice Requirements" on page 110.)

Placement of the notice

Earlier copyright laws carefully regulated the placement of the notice. The 1976 law is more flexible:

> The notice shall be affixed to the copies in such manner and location as to give reasonable notice of the claim of copyright. The Register of Copyrights shall prescribe by regulation, as examples, specific methods of affixation and positions of the notice on various types of works that will satisfy this requirement, but these specifications shall not be considered exhaustive.[2]

The format and placement of the notice on sculpture, jewelry, and other works of art has been a source of controversy. There has been very little controversy about the placement of the notice in printed and audiovisual works. On the basis of earlier legislation, common practices, and the proposed rules issued by the Copyright Office, the locations shown in figure 7 should meet the requirements.

Registration

Registration is required to institute a suit for an infringement. It is also necessary to record an assignment. Works published before January 1, 1978, must be registered prior to renewal for the second term of copyright protection. Musical compositions must be registered to receive the compulsory license fees from record manufacturers.

Materials	Recommended locations*
Works in book form	The title page, page after title page, first page, last page, or either side of the front or back covers
Audiovisual and television programs	The title or credit frames, or immediately following the beginning of the program, or immediately preceding the end of the program
Microform	The first frame, title frame, or frame after the title frame; or (readable without magnification) the heading or border
Photographs, maps, and graphic works	The front or back of the work, or on the matting or frame
Sculptural works	At any visible point on the work or the base of the work
Phonograph records	The center label
Audiocassettes	The body of the cassette
Computer programs	Displayed on the screen at sign-on, or continuous screen display, or on the label of the cartridge, cassette, reel, or container

*Adapted from "Proposed Rulemaking: Methods of Affixation and Positions of the Copyright Notice," Federal Register, *December 23, 1977, pp. 64374-78.*

Fig. 7. Placement of the copyright notice

Registrations are made on official Copyright Office forms.[3] The forms are available without charge from the Copyright Office, Library of Congress, Washington, D.C. 20559. The forms are accompanied by a pamphlet describing registration procedures. When requesting forms, specify the type of materials to be registered. The following categories are now used:

Form TX: for published and unpublished nondramatic literary works

Form PA: for published and unpublished works of the performing arts (musical and dramatic works, pantomimes and choreographic works, motion pictures and other audiovisual works)

Form VA: for published and unpublished works of the visual arts (pictorial, graphic, and sculptural works)

Form SR: for published and unpublished sound recordings

Form RE: for claims to renewal of copyright in works copyrighted under the old law

Two other forms are provided for special situations:

Form CA: for supplementary registration to correct or amplify information given in an earlier registration

Form GR/CP: an adjunct application to be used for registration of a group of contributions to periodicals

Registrations must be accompanied by a check or money order for $10.[4] Deposit accounts are available. Registrations also must be accompanied by one or two deposit copies of the work.

Deposit

A copyright owner must deposit two copies of the best edition of a work in the Copyright Office within three months of publication. (A single copy is required for unpublished works, works published abroad, and contributions to collective works.) Depositing two copies can be an economic burden for the publishers of certain types of works. This is especially true in the case of expensive works and works with a limited distribution. In the past, the Copyright Office and the Library of Congress developed a *modus vivendi* to reduce the deposit burden for filmmakers. Filmmakers deposited two copies of their films in the customary fashion. After completing a simple agreement with the Library of Congress, one or both copies of the films were returned to the filmmaker. The new law provides a more straightforward approach to solving this problem. Copyright Office exemptions include documentation in lieu of deposit and single-copy deposits.

Documentation accepted in lieu of deposit

Diagrams and models of scientific and technical works.

Linear or three-dimensional models of scientific or technical information.

Anatomical models.

Greeting cards, picture postcards, and stationery.

Lectures, sermons, speeches, and addresses when published separately and not in a collection.

Computer programs and automated data bases published in the U.S. only in machine-readable copies.

Three-dimensional sculptural works, including jewelry, dolls, toys, games, and plaques. (Globes and relief maps are not included in this group.)

Tests and answer materials for tests when published separately from other works. (This has special application to standard tests of achievement and ability.)

Works first published as individual contributions to collective works. (The publisher of the collective work must deposit two copies of the work.)

Separately copyrighted sound tracks of motion pictures.

Motion pictures that consist of television transmission programs that have been published only by reason of a license or grant to a nonprofit institution to copy the programs off the air.

Large objects having a single dimension of ninety-six or more inches.

Single-copy deposits

Motion pictures. (The copy must be accompanied by the script, continuity, pressbook, or synopsis. Unless selected by the Library of Congress for its collection, the copy will be returned to the depositor.)

Limited editions of five copies or 300 numbered copies. (Photographs or other identifying materials may be substituted for the single copy under the terms of Copyright Office regulation 202.21.)

Multimedia kits.

Globes, relief maps, and other three-dimensional cartographic representations.

Failure to register or deposit copies

Accidental or deliberate failure to register a work or deposit copies does not remove or diminish copyright protection in a work.[5] The 1909 copyright law stipulated that copies had to be deposited promptly after the work was published. Deposit was essential for obtaining copyright protection. The Supreme Court voided this provision in 1939 because of vagueness in the wording of the law.[6] As a result, it was only necessary to include a proper notice in a work to obtain copyright protection. This practice was incorporated in the 1976 copyright act. In writing the new copyright law, neither Congress nor the Copyright Office wanted to dismantle the registration and deposit apparatus. Orderly registration records are important for determining the ownership of works and the duration of copyright protection. They are essential to the complicated legal affairs of the publishing, music, and film industries. The deposit copies may be used to determine that the work exists as claimed in the registration papers. They are also valuable for building the collections of the Library of Congress, the National Library of Medicine, the National Agricultural Library, the District of Columbia Public Library, and other libraries.

The new copyright law contains a practical compromise in this matter. Registration and deposit are not required to obtain copyright in a work, but they provide a number of crucial advantages. The advantages apply chiefly to litigation. A suit for infringement may not be instituted prior to registration. An owner who properly registers a work within five years of publication is assured that the registration certificate will be honored as *prima facie* evidence of the validity of the copyright. In the event of a successful court action for an infringement, the court may assess the defendant for the plaintiff's attorney's fees and costs, and statutory damages. Under the new law, this can only take place if the plaintiff completed the registration and deposit procedures within three months of the publication of the work. These are substantial advantages.

In spite of these advantages, many individuals and educational institutions do not register their works or deposit copies. They regard the copyright notice as sufficient protection for their pamphlets, lesson plans, bibliographies, advertising brochures, television programs, and so on. They do not anticipate that they will ever institute a suit for an infringement, so they are willing to forego their courtroom advantages in return for the savings accrued in omitting registration and deposit.

The Copyright Office may force copyright owners to comply with the deposit process. If the Copyright Office is aware that a work was published with a notice, it can require the deposit by sending a written notice to the copyright owner. If the copyright owner complies within three months, there is no penalty or forfeiture. If the owner fails to comply within three months, the Copyright Office may levy a fine of up to $250 and a fee equal to the retail price of the work or the cost of acquiring it. Copyright owners who repeatedly or willfully fail to pay the $250 fine may be assessed an additional $2,500 fine.[7]

Special copyright notice requirements

Sound recordings

The copyright notice on phonograph records and tape recordings consists of (1) the letter P in a circle, (2) the name (or a recognized abbreviation of the name) of the copyright owner, and (3) the date of first publication. A typical notice might read ℗ Boston University 1978 or ℗ John Hamilton 1978. The names of institutions may be shortened or abbreviated for convenience. The name of the Champaign Public Library and Information Center might be shortened to Champaign Pub Lib & Info Cntr, or merely to Champaign Pub Lib. The notice should be placed "on the surface of the phonorecord, or on the phonorecord label or container, in such manner and location as to give reasonable notice of the claim of copyright."[8] Figure 7, on page 106, identifies suitable locations for the notice.

Works made for hire

A work made for hire is "a work produced by an employee within the scope of his or her employment. . . ."[9] A teacher, librarian, or instructional specialist who produces bibliographies, instructional materials, sound recordings, or films as a part of his or her employment does not own the copyright in the work; the ownership rests with the employer. The copyright notices in these works should include the employer's name as the copyright owner. (Employees may claim rights to works made for hire by including a provision to that effect in the employment contract.) Works made for hire may also include contributions to collective works (encyclopedias, audiovisual programs, periodicals, supplementary materials) produced on contract, "if the parties expressly agree in a written instrument signed by them that the work shall be considered a work made for hire."[10]

A single copyright notice in a collective work provides adequate protection for the contributions of the various contributors. If the copyright was not transferred to the publisher, the publisher has only the "privilege of reproducing and distributing the contributions as part of that particular collective work, any revision of that collective work, and any later collective work in the same series."[11]

To sum up this complex matter, the copyright notice in a collective work should identify the publisher or editor as the copyright owner. The ownership of the individual contributions is determined by the contract signed between the creator and the publisher. If the individual contributors did not transfer their copyrights to the publisher, their rights are protected, even if their names do not appear in the copyright notice. An individual copyright notice on each contribution is unnecessary.

Joint works

If the coauthors of a work wish to retain the copyright in their own names, the name of each coauthor should appear in the notice. The requirements for copyright notices in works of joint authorship should not be confused with copyright notices in collective works. The author of a contribution to a collective work may retain the copyright in the contribution, even though the publisher's name appears in the copyright notice. This does not apply to joint works.

Works incorporating U.S. government publications

U.S. government publications are in the public domain and may be duplicated without the permission of the author or publisher. The new copyright law imposes new requirements for copyright notices in works incorporating substantial parts of government publications:

> Whenever a work is published in copies or phonorecords consisting
> preponderantly of one or more works of the United States
> Government, the notice of copyright . . . shall also include a
> statement identifying, either affirmatively or negatively, those
> portions . . . embodying any work or works protected under this
> title.[12]

This requirement is aimed at certain segments of the publishing industry, including publishers of legal works, who reprint all or large parts of government publications. They often add an introduction or commentary to the work and then claim copyright protection for the entire work. Under the new law, they must identify those parts included in or excluded from copyright protection. This does not apply to quotations from government publications incorporated in works of original authorship.

Errors and omissions in the notice

Omission of name or date

A work that is legitimately sold or distributed by the authority of the copyright owner and does not contain a name or date in the notice "is considered to have been published without any notice. . . ."[13] However, the copyright owner's initials or some other generally known designation may be substituted for the full name. This is an important consideration for copyright notices on jewelry, decorative objects, or works of art. The year may be omitted in notices on greeting cards, postcards, stationery, jewelry, dolls, toys, or other useful articles.[14] Prior to 1978, the date also could be omitted from maps.

Error in date

When the year date in the notice on copies or phonorecords distributed by authority of the copyright owner is earlier than the year in which publication first occurred, any period computed from the year of first publication . . . is to be computed from the year in the notice. Where the year date is more than one year later than the year in which publication first occurred, the work is considered to have been published without any notice. . . .[15]

Omission of entire notice

The omission of the notice from copies publicly distributed by the authority of the copyright owner does not invalidate the copyright in the work if:

(1) the notice has been omitted from no more than a relatively small number of copies or phonorecords distributed to the public; or
(2) registration for the work has been made before or is made within five years after the publication without notice, and a reasonable effort is made to add notice to all copies or phonorecords that are distributed to the public in the United States after the omission has been discovered; or

(3) the notice has been omitted in violation of an express requirement in writing that, as a condition of the copyright owner's authorization of the public distribution of copies or phonorecords they bear the prescribed notice.[16]

This section was included in the new copyright law to mitigate the severe penalties previously associated with accidental omission of the notice in a few copies of a work. However, a person who finds a copy without a copyright notice "incurs no liability for actual or statutory damages . . . for any infringing acts committed before receiving actual notice that" the work was protected by a legitimate copyright.[17]

Copyright protection "is not affected by the removal, destruction, or obliteration of the notice . . . from any publicly distributed copies. . . ."[18]

Copyright renewal

Under the 1909 copyright law, copyright protection lasted for twenty-eight years. It could be renewed in the twenty-eighth year for an additional term of twenty-eight years. The new copyright law did not remove the renewal requirements for works published before January 1, 1978. These must still be renewed in the twenty-eighth year. Renewal consists of submitting a properly completed renewal form and a six-dollar fee to the Copyright Office. Renewal forms and a pamphlet describing the renewal process are available free of charge from the Copyright Office, Library of Congress, Washington, D.C. 20559. The new law made one important change in the renewal process. Renewal now extends the duration of copyright protection by forty-seven years, thus providing seventy-five years of copyright protection for these works.

Appendixes

Contents

Appendix A

Agreement on guidelines
for classroom copying in not-for-profit
educational institutions with respect to books and periodicals*

The purpose of the following guidelines is to state the minimum standards of educational fair use under Section 107 of H.R. 2223. The parties agree that the conditions determining the extent of permissible copying for educational purposes may change in the future; that certain types of copying permitted under these guidelines may not be permissible in the future; and conversely that in the future other types of copying not permitted under these guidelines may be permissible under revised guidelines.

Moreover, the following statement of guidelines is not intended to limit the types of copying permitted under the standards of fair use under judicial decision and which are stated in Section 107 of the Copyright Revision Bill. There may be instances in which copying which does not fall within the guidelines stated below may nonetheless be permitted under the criteria of fair use.

Guidelines

I. *Single Copying for Teachers*

A single copy may be made of any of the following by or for a teacher at his or her individual request for his or her scholarly research or use in teaching or preparation to teach a class:

A. A chapter from a book;

B. An article from a periodical or newspaper;

C. A short story, short essay or short poem, whether or not from a collective work;

D. A chart, graph, diagram, drawing, cartoon or picture from a book, periodical, or newspaper;

II. *Multiple Copies for Classroom Use*

Multiple copies (not to exceed in any event more than one copy per pupil in a course) may be made by or for the teacher giving the course for classroom use or discussion; *provided that:*

A. The copying meets the tests of brevity and spontaneity as defined below; *and,*

B. Meets the cumulative effect test as defined below; *and,*

C. Each copy includes a notice of copyright.

Definitions

Brevity

(*i*) Poetry: (a) A complete poem if less than 250 words and if printed on not more than two pages, or (b) from a longer poem, an excerpt of not more than 250 words.

*U.S. House of Representatives, Report No. 94-1476, Sec. 107.

116

(*ii*) Prose: (a) Either a complete article, story or essay of less than 2,500 words, or (b) an excerpt from any prose work of not more than 1,000 words or 10% of the work, whichever is less, but in any event a minimum of 500 words.

[Each of the numerical limits stated in "i" and "ii" above may be expanded to permit the completion of an unfinished line of a poem or of an unfinished prose paragraph.]

(*iii*) Illustration: One chart, graph, diagram, drawing, cartoon or picture per book or per periodical issue.

(*iv*) "Special" works: Certain works in poetry, prose or in "poetic prose" which often combine language with illustrations and which are intended sometimes for children and at other times for a more general audience fall short of 2,500 words in their entirety. Paragraph "ii" above notwithstanding such "special works" may not be reproduced in their entirety; however, an excerpt comprising not more than two of the published pages of such special work and containing not more than 10% of the words found in the text thereof, may be reproduced.

Spontaneity

(*i*) The copying is at the instance and inspiration of the individual teacher, and

(*ii*) The inspiration and decision to use the work and the moment of its use for maximum teaching effectiveness are so close in time that it would be unreasonable to expect a timely reply to a request for permission.

Cumulative Effect

(*i*) The copying of the material is for only one course in the school in which the copies are made.

(*ii*) Not more than one short poem, article, story, essay or two excerpts may be copied from the same author, nor more than three from the same collective work or periodical volume during one class term.

(*iii*) There shall not be more than nine instances of such multiple copying for one course during one class term.

[The limitations stated in "ii" and "iii" above shall not apply to current news periodicals and newspapers and current news sections of other periodicals.]

III. *Prohibitions as to I and II Above*

Notwithstanding any of the above, the following shall be prohibited:

(A) Copying shall not be used to create or to replace or substitute for anthologies, compilations or collective works. Such replacement or substitution may occur whether copies of various works or excerpts therefrom are accumulated or reproduced and used separately.

(B) There shall be no copying of or from works intended to be "consumable" in the course of study or of teaching. These include workbooks, exercises, standardized tests and test booklets and answer sheets and like consumable material.

(C) Copying shall not:

(a) substitute for the purchase of books, publishers' reprints or periodicals;

(b) be directed by higher authority;

(c) be repeated with respect to the same item by the same teacher from term to term.

(D) No charge shall be made to the student beyond the actual cost of the photocopying.

Agreed March 19, 1976.

Ad Hoc Committee on Copyright Law Revision:

By Sheldon Elliott Steinbach.

Author-Publisher Group:
Authors League of America:

By Irwin Karp, *Counsel.*

Association of American Publishers, Inc.:

By Alexander C. Hoffman,
Chairman, Copyright Committee.

Appendix B
Joint statement of policy on school rerecording of public and instructional television programs

November 1975

With the increased capability for off-air rerecording of educationally useful television programs for replay at times convenient to classroom scheduling, it is important to school systems that public and instructional programs be available for classroom playback, closed-circuit display and other school exhibition modes contemporaneously with local station broadcast. Content copyright and other legal limitations, however, often demand that the use of such program rerecordings be controlled in a manner consistent with original television broadcast authorization.

Accordingly, the below signatory agencies have jointly agreed on the general policy of authorizing supplemental school rerecordings of public and instructional television programs distributed by them for local ETV and other educational broadcast, solely on condition that:

1. School rerecordings may be made only by students, teachers, and faculty or staff members in an accredited non-profit educational institution;
2. School rerecordings will be used solely for classroom, auditorium or laboratory exhibition in the course of classroom instruction or related educational activities;
3. School rerecordings will be used only in the educational institution for which made, and will not be given away, loaned or otherwise made available outside that educational institution;
4. School rerecordings will be used only during the seven-day period of local ETV and other educational broadcast licensed by the distribution agency, and will be erased or destroyed immediately at the end of that seven-day period except to the extent specifically authorized in writing in advance by the distribution agency.

The signatory agencies have agreed that this supplemental school rerecording authorization will be applicable to all public and instructional programs distributed by them, excluding only those prohibited by reason of production or distribution rights restrictions.

Public Broadcasting Service   Public Television Library

Great Plains National Instructional   Agency for Instructional
Television Library   Television

Appendix C
The Agency for Instructional Television's extended retention policy

April 28, 1976

All AIT telecourses are available for off-air recording by schools as stated in the Joint Policy on "School Rerecording of Public and Instructional Television Programs" issued by PBS/PTL, GPNITL and AIT on November 15, 1975. An important condition of the Joint Policy, however, is that such school rerecordings can be used only during the seven-day period of station broadcast and then must be erased.

In response to numerous requests from school districts across the country, AIT is taking a further step toward making its telecourses—all of which are specifically designed for classroom use—even more accessible to schools. Beginning September 1, 1976, agencies authorized to use AIT telecourses may, on an experimental basis, permit their participating school systems to retain rerecordings for repeated use as desired during the entire school year, September through June.

The aim of this experiment is to test the extent to which unrestricted broadcast rerecordings will be used in classrooms. A further objective is to determine if such an extended use will increase school support for instructional broadcast services. Finally, it is hoped the experiment will provide insight into the effect of advances in recording and playback technology upon instructional broadcasting.

The AIT experiment is for a three-year period (September, 1976 through June, 1979). It will be confined to telecourses for which AIT controls distribution rights in all recording formats (i.e., film, videotape, reel-to-reel, videocassette, videodisc, etc.) and for all exhibition methods (i.e., television transmission, classroom playback, film projector, closed-circuit systems, etc.). The experiment also will be limited to school systems specifically identified as participants in the instructional television services of agencies authorized to use AIT telecourses. Non-participating school systems will still not be authorized to exceed the seven-day recording retention limit of the Joint Policy on "School Rerecording of Public and Instructional Television Programs."

Appendix D

The National Commission on the New Technological Uses of Copyrighted Works (CONTU) guidelines for the proviso of subsection 108(G)(2)

1. As used in the proviso of subsection 108(G)(2), the words ". . . such aggregate quantities as to substitute for a subscription to or purchase of such work" shall mean:

   (a) with respect to any given periodical (as opposed to any given issue of a periodical), filled requests of a library or archives (a "requesting entity") within any calendar year for a total of six or more copies of an article or articles published in such periodical within five years prior to the date of the request. These guidelines specifically shall not apply, directly or indirectly, to any request of a requesting entity for a copy or copies of an article or articles published in any issue of a periodical, the publication date of which is more than five years prior to the date when the request is made. These guidelines do not define the meaning, with respect to such a request, of ". . . such aggregate quantities as to substitute for a subscription to [such periodical]."

   (b) with respect to any other material described in subsection 108(d), (including fiction and poetry), filled requests of a requesting entity within any calendar year for a total of six or more copies or phonorecords of or from any given work (including a collective work) during the entire period when such material shall be protected by copyright.

2. In the event that a requesting entity—

   (a) shall have in force or shall have entered an order for a subscription to a periodical, or

   (b) has within its collection, or shall have entered an order for, a copy or phonorecord of any other copyrighted work,

   material from either category of which it desires to obtain by copy from another library or archives (the "supplying entity"), because the material to be copied is not reasonably available for use by the requesting entity itself, then the fulfillment of such request shall be treated as though the requesting entity made such copy from its own collection. A library or archives may request a copy or phonorecord from a supplying entity only under those circumstances where the requesting entity would have been able, under the other provisions of section 108, to supply such copy from materials in its own collection.

3. No request for a copy or phonorecord of any material to which these guidelines apply may be fulfilled by the supplying entity unless such request is accompanied by a representation by the requesting entity that the request was made in conformity with these guidelines.

4. The requesting entity shall maintain records of all requests made by it for copies or phonorecords of any materials to which these guidelines apply and shall maintain records of the fulfillment of such requests, which records shall be retained until the end of the third complete calendar year after the end of the calendar year in which the respective request shall have been made.

5. As part of the review provided for in subsection 108(i), these guidelines shall be reviewed not later than five years from the effective date of this bill.

Appendix E
Final report of Working Group I:
Conference on Video Recording for Educational Uses,
July 19-22, 1977*

1. *The present dimensions of the problem.* Group I recognized that a great deal of off-the-air taping for educational purposes is currently going on, although one member of the group felt that some estimates of its general pervasiveness were exaggerated. Most of the taping activities take place within educational institutions on the institutions' own equipment, and is either done by teachers or at their instance. For the most part it is not inaccurate to describe the practices as spontaneous, though there are some notable exceptions. Similarly, there is little duplication or use of the tapes outside the educational institution where they were made. There is less off-the-air taping for educational purposes in the lower grades, with the curve rising at the secondary, college, and university levels. The types of programs taped, and the varieties of teaching purposes to which the tapes are put, covered an almost unlimited range. There is little pattern to the various lengths of time tapes are kept before being erased; some may be kept for several years or even indefinitely, and dissatisfaction was expressed by educators with respect to the "seven-day" rule now in use to some extent in educational broadcasting. Organized licensing practices that meet educators' needs to tape off the air or to obtain copies of television programs for classroom use are, with some exceptions, either nonexistent or are not operating very efficiently.

2. *Future possibilities.* Group I agreed that off-air taping of television programs was certain to continue and to increase substantially, but beyond this it regarded definite predictions as risky. An important but uncertain factor was whether videotape or the video disk would eventually become the dominant form for video-recordings; if disks (with playback but without recording possibilities) achieve market dominance, the copyright owners' control over use of their works would be enhanced. However, the introduction of any form of low-cost video recordings into the consumer market on a large scale seems likely to have a radical effect on traditional forms of broadcasting, programming, and advertising, and to impel copyright owners to take action to defend themselves against unauthorized recording. The Group considered that efforts to introduce jamming signals into programming to impede its taping would be subject to strong criticism and would be likely to prove futile.

The final conference report had not been issued at the time the manuscript for this book left the author's hands.

3. *General views*

a. Working Group I as a whole did not accept the view that off-air taping should be free of copyright restrictions in all cases and under all circumstances, nor did it accept the opposite view that unauthorized off-the-air taping should be considered copyright infringement in every case, without regard to the doctrine of fair use. One member of the Group felt that, at least philosophically, there should be no restrictions on off-air taping for nonprofit educational purposes. A representative of organized performers, while not ruling out the possibility of applying the fair use doctrine to off-air taping in certain cases, was constrained not to discuss general guidelines for fair use in this area, at least until after licensing procedures had been worked out.

b. Within Group I there was no expressed opposition to the making of off-air recording by libraries for archival preservation, or to the use of the tapes by individual scholars for research purposes, under the fair use doctrine. The librarians on the Group expressed the need for clearer guidelines as to the meaning of fair use in this area. The Group agreed that a distinction must be drawn between archival preservation and research use on the one hand, and use of tapes in classroom teaching on the other.

4. *Fair use*

a. With the exception of one member representing organized performers, Group I concluded that there are fair use principles applicable to off-the-air taping for educational purposes, and that the extent to which a work can be used under the fair use doctrine without payment should be considered before attempting to define the procedures for clearance, licensing, and payment for uses beyond fair use. The need for eventual guidelines governing specific practices permitted and prohibited as fair use was recognized. Educators in Group I agreed that teachers want to know the applicable principles so they can abide by them.

b. At the same time, it was noted that the breadth or narrowness of the fair use definition will interact with whatever licensing procedure is agreed upon beyond fair use. Where clearances are necessary beyond fair use, educators want simple, efficient, and effective licensing procedures that will allow them timely access to the material they need.

c. With the exception already noted, Group I determined that the following principles are worthy of discussion within the various groups and interests affected by off-air taping for educational purposes, and of further consideration among these groups and interests:

(1) It is essential to define the limits of fair use for educational

purposes as the first priority. This definition should precede consideration of licensing. Licensing would apply only to the use of audiovisual materials beyond the permitted fair use.

(2) The definition of fair use should include the privilege to reproduce televised works off-the-air in whole or in part, and to retain and use these reproductions in noncommercial classroom situations and in other systematic noncommercial instructional activities, for teaching purposes, for a limited period of time.

(3) Where an entire work is reproduced, the appropriate credits and the copyright notice should be included in all cases. Where an excerpt is reproduced, the work from which it is taken should be identified, and the copyright notice should be reproduced unless impracticable (e.g., stock footage).

(4) The following practices would be prohibited under the doctrine of fair use:

(a) the making of more than a single copy by or for a particular teacher;

(b) any transfer, distribution or use of the copy made under the fair use doctrine outside the educational institution;

(c) reproduction of "theatrical" or "feature" films (i.e., films previously distributed for public showing other than on television), inasmuch as these are available through licensing arrangements for educational use.

(d) off-air taping of broadcasts by an educational institution, not at the specific instance of an individual teacher.

(5) Duplication or multiplication of additional copies of a work by or for the same teacher would not come within the doctrine of fair use.

(6) There was general agreement that tapes made under the fair use doctrine should be erased at the end of a limited period, but the Group reached no conclusion as to what that period should be, and agreed that more exploration is needed as to the availability of licenses and patterns of use. Various possibilities were discussed: a period based on "school days"; on a particular number of classes scheduled in a course; on the length of a curricular unit such as a semester or quarter; or on the number of uses. The Group was unable to agree as to whether the relevant period should start from the first broadcast of a particular program on television, or from any broadcast, even if a rerun. There was some interest in the possibility of having variable standards based on whether, at the time of a rerun, the program was available for licensing.

(7) There was general acceptance of the principle that any guidelines worked out should be enforced, to the extent possible, by the authorities of the educational institution involved, but no consensus

was achieved as to what this would mean in practice as to record-keeping and active policing.

(8) There was some feeling that the standard of spontaneity was an important factor in applying the doctrine of fair use, and that this had bearing on the length of time a tape could be retained and used before erasure. The Group as a whole, however, did not adopt a definition of spontaneity as a basic requirement of fair use in this area.

(9) It was agreed that off-air taping for purposes of archival preservation and for research use in libraries and archives comes within the doctrine of fair use. However, it was not agreed that the presence of tapes in an archive available to teachers carries with it the privilege to use the tape for classroom teaching purposes.

5. *Licensing procedures*
   a. There was no support among Working Group I for alternative approaches to licensing of educational taping beyond fair use, such as tax credits or levies on tape recorders or tapes.
   b. At the present time, there were no members of Group I advocating any sort of compulsory licensing scheme, although the educators did not rule out the possibility for the future. Instead, the Group saw a pressing need for a central organization from which educators could readily obtain information about clearances and through which licensing arrangements could be made. Educators were primarily concerned about uniformity, ease and efficiency of access, and reasonableness of fees; the view was expressed that producers generally should work toward licensing in large enough quantities to allow the economics of scale to bring fees down to a level educators can pay.

Barbara Ringer, Leader
Marlene Morrisey, Rapporteur

American Library Association
record maintenance and retention guidelines
for interlibrary loan departments

This statement deals only with recommended RECORD MAINTENANCE
AND RETENTION GUIDELINES. Interlibrary Loan librarians have a
responsibility to familiarize themselves thoroughly with the provisions of
the Copyright Revision Act of 1976 (P.L. 94-553), particularly Sections
107 and 108, and the provisions of the Guidelines drafted by the National
Commission on New Technological Uses of Copyrighted Works (CONTU).
Guideline #4 states:

> The requesting entity shall maintain records of all requests made by it
> for copies or phonorecords of any materials to which these guidelines
> apply and shall maintain records of the fulfillment of such requests,
> which records shall be retained until the end of the third complete
> calendar year after the end of the calendar year in which the
> respective request shall have been made.

Most libraries already keep some kind of record of *all* interlibrary loan requests. That record should continue. However, it must be supplemented
by the kind of record described below *for certain kinds of requests.* (See
Subsection 108(d) of the law and CONTU Guideline #1)

1. *Form of Record.*
   It is recommended that records for periodicals be kept by title. Two
   possibilities seem workable: 1) a copy of the ALA Request for Loan
   or Photocopy form, a copy of the teletype request, etc. could be kept;
   or 2) a card could be set up for each title requested containing essential information including whatever is necessary to link this card to
   the library's file of request forms.

   N.B.: A library may choose one of these methods or develop its own.
   Whatever is done it is essential that the library keep a file of requests
   for these materials, that the file be accessible by title and that the date
   of the request be noted.

2. *Creation of Record.*
   a. For periodical material: Beginning on January 1, 1978, when a
      request is made for a copy of an article or articles published in a
      copyrighted periodical *within five years prior to the date of the re-
      quest,* the library will either: a) set up a card for the title of that
      periodical or b) enter a copy of the request form in a file of forms
      arranged by title. If a card is set up it should include the date of
      the request and either the name of the requester or the requester's
      order number so that reference may be made to the complete form

if necessary. All later requests for the same periodical title will be recorded in like manner.

    b. For material in any other copyrighted work: Beginning on January 1, 1978, when a request is made for a contribution to a collection or for a small part of any copyrighted work, the library will follow procedures based on those described above. The record may be kept by title or main entry.

3. *Use of Record.*

    a. Making requests: Before requesting a photocopy, the record will be checked. If a library is using the card system and no card exists, one will be created. If a card does exist, and the number of previous requests filled complies with the CONTU Guidelines, the date and name of requester will be entered. If a library is using the copy system and the number of previous requests complies with the CONTU Guidelines, the request will be made and a copy filed.

    b. Receiving material: When a request is filled, this will be noted on the card or copy. If a request is not filled, a line will be drawn through the entry on the card or the copy will be marked "not filled."

4. *Contingencies.*

When a request is made for loan of material rather than a copy, but the supplying library sends a photocopy, a record will be made either by marking on a card or by filing a copy of the form, at the time when the material is *received.*

5. *Retention of Records.*

    a. Items in this file of cards or copies of forms must be kept until the end of the third complete calendar year after the end of the calendar year in which a request shall have been made. Thus, for a request made on any date in 1978, the record must be retained until 31 December 1981.

    b. If a library uses the card method, copies of the form on which an interlibrary loan has been requested must also be kept, in whatever order the library wishes, until the end of the third complete calendar year after the end of the calendar year in which a request is made.

    c. Information contained in the records should be summarized before records are destroyed. The summary may be useful for the five-year review mandated by Subsection 108(i) of the copyright law as well as for internal management purposes. Suggestions for the form of the five-year review summary will be made at a later time.

American Library Association
Reference and Adult Services Division
Interlibrary Loan Committee
September, 1977

Appendix G
Guidelines for educational uses of music

The purpose of the following guidelines is to state the minimum and not the maximum standards of educational fair use under Section 107 of HR 2223. The parties agree that the conditions determining the extent of permissible copying for educational purposes may change in the future; that certain types of copying permitted under these guidelines may not be permissible in the future, and conversely that in the future other types of copying not permitted under these guidelines may not be permissible under revised guidelines.

Moreover, the following statement of guidelines is not intended to limit the types of copying permitted under the standards of fair use under judicial decision and which are stated in Section 107 of the Copyright Revision Bill. There may be instances in which copying which does not fall within the guidelines stated below may nonetheless be permitted under the criteria of fair use.

A. *Permissible Uses*
1. Emergency copying to replace purchased copies which for any reason are not available for an imminent performance provided purchased replacement copies shall be substituted in due course.
2. (a) For academic purposes other than performance, multiple copies of excerpts of works may be made, provided that the excerpts do not comprise a part of the whole which would constitute a performable unit such as a selection, movement or aria, but in no case more than 10% of the whole work. The number of copies shall not exceed one copy per pupil.
   (b) For academic purposes other than performance, a single copy of an entire performable unit (section, movement, aria, etc.) that is (1) confirmed by the copyright proprietor to be out of print, or (2) unavailable except in a larger work, may be made by or for a teacher solely for the purpose of his or her scholarly research or in preparation to teach a class.
3. Printed copies which have been purchased may be edited or simplified provided that the fundamental character of the work is not distorted or the lyrics, if any, altered or lyrics added if none exist.
4. A single copy of recordings of performances by students may be made for evaluation or rehearsal purposes and may be retained by the educational institution or individual teacher.
5. A single copy of a sound recording (such as a tape, disc or cassette) of copyrighted music may be made from sound recordings owned by an educational institution or an individual teacher for the purpose of constructing aural exercises or examinations and may be retained by the educational institution or individual teacher. (This

pertains only to the copyright of the music itself and not to any copyright which may exist in the sound recording.)

B. *Prohibitions*

1. Copying to create or replace or substitute for anthologies, compilations or collective works.
2. Copying of or from works intended to be "consumable" in the course of study or of teaching such as workbooks, exercises, standardized tests and answer sheets and like material.
3. Copying for the purpose of performance, except as in A(1) above.
4. Copying for the purpose of substituting for the purchase of music, except as in A(1) and A(2) above.
5. Copying without inclusion of the copyright notice which appears on the printed copy.

Appendix H
American Library Association
guidelines for seeking or making a copy
of an entire copyrighted work
for a library, archives, or user

A library or archives which wishes to make a single photocopy or sound recording copy of a published copyrighted work for a user or to replace a copy or phonorecord in its collection which is damaged, deteriorating, lost, or stolen, must first make a reasonable effort to obtain a copy in its original form at a fair price, in accordance with Subsections 108(c) and 108(e) of Public Law 94-553, the 1976 omnibus copyright revision act.

"Reasonable Effort"

A reasonable effort requires that the library or archives take the following steps:

1. Attempt to determine whether the work is in print by consulting commonly-known trade bibliographic sources, e.g., *Publishers' Trade List Annual, Books in Print* for printed books, *Schwann Catalog, Phonolog* for phonorecords.
2. If the work is in print, attempt to acquire it from a library wholesaler or retail outlet, or from the publisher of the work.
3. If the work is out of print and unavailable in its original form from these sources, attempt to acquire the work or a photocopy or sound recording copy from the publisher or other copyright owner (if such owner can be located readily at the address listed in the copyright registration) or from an authorized reproducing service.
4. If the publisher, other copyright owner, or authorized reproducing service is unable or unwilling to supply a copy of the work, or if the requesting library receives no reply to its request within thirty days of the date it is sent, then it may place an order for a photocopy or sound recording copy with a library or archives which has a copy.* The "Revised Interlibrary Loan Form," which has been prepared by the ALA-RASD Interlibrary Loan Committee, may be used for this purpose, in

---

Author's comment: The legality of this sentence is open to serious question. Sections 108(c) and (e) place the burden of "a reasonable effort" and "a reasonable investigation" on the library that attempts to replace a damaged copy or an out-of-print work. The law does not comment on the responsibility of the copyright owner or the vendor to provide good services. Inasmuch as the law places the entire burden on libraries, it requires a considerable stretch of the imagination to interpret this section in a manner that permits libraries to unilaterally impose thirty-day fulfillment requirements on the copyright owner or the reproduction service. A library should not implement this part of the guidelines without consulting its attorney. For further information about unilaterally imposed requirements, see pages 95-98.

which case the appropriate box on the form should be checked, to indicate that all of the above-mentioned steps have been taken. An order form used in its stead should also indicate compliance with these guidelines.

"Fair Price"

1. *Original format*

   In order to meet the requirement of fair price, an unused copy of a published copyrighted work should be available at a price as close as possible to the latest suggested retail price.

2. *Reproductions* (photocopy, microform, sound recording copy)

   To meet the requirement of fair price, a reproduction of a copyrighted work should be available on a timely basis (within thirty days) at a price which is as close as possible to actual manufacturing costs plus royalty payments.*

The requesting library or archives shall maintain records on all requests it has made for photocopies or sound recording copies to which these guidelines apply, together with records of the fulfillment of these requests, which records shall be retained until the end of the third complete calendar year after the end of the calendar year in which the respective request shall have been made.

Authorized Reproducing Services

The House Judiciary Committee Report on the New Copyright Law (H. Rept. 94-1476) in discussing Subsections 108(c) and 108(e) of the copyright law, specifies that a reasonable investigation to determine that an unused replacement or copy cannot be obtained at a fair price will, in the normal situation, involve recourse to the publisher or other copyright owner, or an authorized reproducing service.

The RTSD [Resources and Technical Services Division of the American Library Association] Copyright Revision Act Committee has prepared a set of criteria which authorized reproducing services should meet in providing adequate services to the library community.

Publishers, other copyright owners, and authorized reproducing services which receive requests for photocopies or sound recording copies should all be required to meet the following conditions:

1. The copy supplied should be of sufficiently good quality to meet the needs of the user, or of as good quality as that which the requesting library or archives could ordinarily expect to receive from any supplier.

---

*Author's comment: See the comment above about the thirty-day fulfillment requirement. It would seem more appropriate to identify a "Fair price" for a reproduction as being as close as possible to the actual manufacturing costs, plus royalties and a reasonable profit.

2. The copy should be supplied, or notification given to the requestor that such copy cannot be supplied, within thirty days of the date of receipt of the request.
3. The price of the copy should be as close as possible to actual manufacturing costs plus royalty payments.

If any of these conditions are not met, the requestor may be considered to have complied with the provisions of Subsections 108(c) and 108(e) of PL 94-553 and may order a photocopy or sound recording of a work from a library or archives which possesses one without further authorization.

While authorized reproducing services should be required to meet the same criteria of quality, service and price as publishers and other copyright owners, there is a great need for better bibliographic information about what titles are available from such reproducing services. This could be done in the following way:

1. Publishers should include in their catalogs in *PTLA* a list of titles which are available from reproducing services and their prices, together with the names and addresses of these services.
2. *Books in Print* should include these titles in their regular listing, together with the names of the reproducing services, or they could have a separate listing of these titles.

Prepared by Implementation of the Copyright Revision Act Committee
Resources and Technical Services Division
American Library Association

Notes

Chapter 1
A brief history of copyright

1. Isaiah Thomas, *The History of Printing in America, With a Biography of Printers & an Account of Newspapers,* edited by Marcus A. McCorison from the second edition. (New York: Weathervane Books, 1970), p. 68.
2. Ibid.
3. *United States Constitution,* Article I, Section 8.
4. U.S. Copyright Act of 1790, Section 5.

Chapter 2
Fair use

1. Saul Cohen, "Fair Use in the Law of Copyright," *Copyright Law Symposium Number Six: Nathan Burkan Memorial Competition Sponsored by the American Society of Composers, Authors and Publishers* (New York: Columbia University Press, 1955), pp. 48-49.
2. Horace G. Ball, *The Law of Copyright and Literary Property* (Albany N.Y.: Banks, 1944), p. 260.
3. *United States Code,* Title 17, "Copyrights," sec. 107. Hereafter cited as Copyright Law.
4. U.S. Senate, *Report No. 94-473,* sec. 107. Hereafter cited as Senate report.
5. Copyright Law, sec. 107.
6. Senate report, sec. 107.

Notes

7. U.S. House of Representatives, *Report No. 94-1476,* sec. 107. Hereafter cited as House report.
8. Association of American Publishers, *Copyright Permissions: A Guide for Non-commercial Use* (Washington, D.C.: The Association, 1975).
9. Senate report, sec. 107.
10. House report, sec. 107.
11. Ibid.
12. Harold E. Wigren, "An Educator's Interpretation of the New Copyright Law, 1977," in *Copyright and the Teaching/Learning Process,* ed. Jerome K. Miller (Pullman, Wash.: Information Futures, 1977), p. 22.
13. Senate report, sec. 107.
14. House report, sec. 107.
15. Senate report, sec. 107.
16. Ibid.
17. Ibid.
18. Ibid.
19. Ibid.
20. House report, sec. 107.
21. Richard Crosby DeWolf, *An Outline of Copyright Law* (Boston: Luce, 1925), p. 143.
22. Cohen, "Fair Use in the Law of Copyright," p. 51.
23. Melville B. Nimmer, *Nimmer on Copyright: A Treatise on the Law of Literary, Musical and Artistic Property, and the Protection of Ideas* (Albany: Bender, 1963-   ), p. 644.
24. Senate report, sec. 107.
25. House report, sec. 107.
26. Senate report, sec. 107.
27. Ibid.
28. Jerome K. Miller, "An Evaluation of Publishers' Responses to Two Procedures Educators and Librarians May Use to Write for Permission to Reproduce Portions of Materials Protected by U.S. Copyright" (Ed.D. diss., University of Colorado, 1976), pp. 55-59.
29. *Nimmer on Copyright,* p. 653.
30. Copyright Law, sec. 110(1).
31. Senate report, sec. 110.
32. Copyright Law, sec. 110(2).
33. Senate report, sec. 110.
34. Ibid.
35. Ibid.
36. Copyright Law, sec. 110(3).
37. Senate report, sec. 110.
38. Copyright Law, sec. 111(4).
39. Senate report, sec. 110.

40. House report, sec. 110.
41. Copyright Law, sec. 110(8).
42. Ibid., sec. 110(9).
43. The best laymen's account of the *CBS* vs. *Vanderbilt* case is found in Cosette Kies, "The Vanderbilt-CBS Litigation: Taping the Evening News," in *Copyright Law, Fair Use and the New Media,* eds. John Shelton Laurence and Bernard Timberg (Norwood, N.J.: Ablex, in press).
44. House report, sec. 107.
45. Copyright Law, sec. 108(f)(3).
46. House report, sec. 108.
47. Copyright Law, sec. 108(a).
48. Robert W. Kastenmeier, [Remarks] *Congressional Record,* Vol. 122 (September 22, 1976), pp. 10874-10875.
49. U.S. House of Representatives, *Report No. 94-1733,* sec. 107. Hereafter cited as Conference report.
50. Copyright Law, sec. 108(c).
51. House report, sec. 108.
52. Copyright Law, sec. 112(b).
53. Senate report, sec. 112.
54. Copyright Law, sec. 101.
55. Senate report, sec. 112.
56. Copyright Law, sec. 118.
57. House report, sec. 118.
58. Ibid., sec. 112.
59. Copyright Law, sec. 112(d).
60. Senate report, sec. 107.
61. Kastenmeier, p. 10874.
62. Conference report, sec. 107.
63. House report, sec. 107.
64. Ibid.
65. Copyright Law, sec. 106.
66. Senate report, sec. 106.
67. Ibid.
68. Copyright Law, sec. 101.
69. Ibid., sec. 109(b)(c).
70. Ibid., sec. 110(1).
71. Ibid., sec. 110(2).
72. House report, sec. 107.
73. Fred W. McDarrah, *Stock Photo and Assignment Source Book* (New York: Bowker, 1977).

Chapter 3
Library photocopying

1. Melville B. Nimmer, *Nimmer on Copyright: A Treatise on the Law of Literary, Musical and Artistic Property, and the Protection of Ideas* (Albany: Bender, 1963-   ), p. 654, n. 210a.
2. Lewis I. Flacks, "An Attorney's Advice to Librarians," *American Libraries* 8, no. 5 (May 1977): 254.
3. *United States Code,* Title 17, "Copyrights," sec. 108(f)(4). Hereafter cited as Copyright Law.
4. Ibid., sec. 108(a)(1).
5. U.S. House of Representatives, *Report No. 94-1476,* sec. 108. Hereafter cited as House report.
6. Ibid.
7. Copyright Law, sec. 108(a)(2).
8. Ibid., sec. 108(a)(3).
9. "Warning Notices for Copies and Machines," *American Libraries* 8, no. 10 (November 1977): 530.
10. Copyright Law, sec. 108(d).
11. Ibid., sec. 108(d)(1).
12. Ibid., sec. 108(d)(2).
13. "Warning of Copyright for Use by Libraries and Archives," *Federal Register,* November 16, 1977, pp. 59264-59265.
14. Ibid.
15. Copyright Law, sec. 108(g).
16. Ibid., sec. 108(h).
17. Ibid., sec. 108(f)(1).
18. "Three Words Added to Copyright Notice," *American Libraries* 9, no. 1 (January 1978): 22.
19. Henry Campbell Black, *Black's Law Dictionary* (St. Paul: West Publishing Co., 1951), p. 1607.
20. Copyright Law, sec. 108(f)(2).
21. Copyright Law, sec. 108(c).
22. House report, sec. 108.
23. Copyright Law, sec. 108(c).
24. American Library Association, Resources and Technical Services Division, Implementation of the Copyright Revision Act Committee, "Guidelines for Seeking or Making a Copy of an Entire Copyrighted Work for a Library, Archives or User" (Chicago: The Committee, no date), unpaged.
25. Copyright Law, sec. 108(g)(2).
26. House report, sec. 108.
27. U.S. National Commission on the New Technological Uses of Copyrighted Works, "Guidelines for the Proviso of Subsection

108(g)(2)" in the U.S. House of Representatives, *Report No. 94-1733,* sec. 108. Hereafter cited as CONTU Guidelines.

28. American Library Association, Reference and Adult Services Division, Interlibrary Loan Committee, "Revised Interlibrary Loan Form" (Chicago: The Association, 1977), unpaged.
29. CONTU Guidelines.
30. Ibid.
31. Copyright Law, sec. 108(i).
32. Ibid., sec. 108(e)(2).
33. House report, sec. 108.
34. *Black's Law Dictionary,* p. 717.
35. Ibid., p. 1721.
36. American Library Association, Resources and Technical Services Division, Implementation of the Copyright Revision Act Committee, "Guidelines for Seeking or Making a Copy of an Entire Copyrighted Work for a Library, Archives or User," unpaged.
37. Copyright Law, sec. 108(b).
38. House report, sec. 108.
39. Copyright Law, sec. 101.
40. Ibid., sec. 108(h).
41. House report, sec. 108.
42. U.S. House of Representatives, *Report No. 94-1733,* sec. 108.
43. Copyright Law, sec. 405(b).
44. U.S. Copyright Office, *Catalog of Copyright Entries: Cumulative Series* (Washington, D.C.: Government Printing Office, 1906-   ).
45. U.S. Copyright Office, "How to Investigate the Copyright Status of a Work" (Washington, D.C.: Copyright Office, 1977).
46. U.S. Private Law, 92-60.
47. Copyright Law, sec. 108(f)(4).
48. A similar interpretation is found in John C. Stedman, "Academic Library Reserves, Photocopying and the Copyright Law" *ALA Washington Newsletter* 30, no. 7 (July 14, 1978), unpaged.
49. House report, sec. 107.

Chapter 4
Obtaining permission

1. *United States Code,* Title 17, "Copyrights" (1909 ed.), sec. 1(e).
2. *United States Code,* Title 17, "Copyrights," sec. 115(c)(2).
3. Ibid., sec. 118(b).
4. Association of American Publishers, TSM Copy Payments Center Task Force, *Program for the Provision of Copies of Technical-Scientific Medical Journal Articles and for Related Information-Service Copying* (New York: The Association, 1977).

5. Association of American Publishers, *Copyright Permissions: A Guide to Non-commercial Use* (New York: The Association, 1975); Association of Media Producers, *Copyright and Educational Media: A Guide to Fair Use and Permissions Procedures* (Washington, D.C.: Association for Educational Communications and Technology, 1977); and Jerome K. Miller, "An Evaluation of Publishers' Responses to Two Procedures Educators and Librarians May Use to Write for Permission to Reproduce Portions of Materials Protected by U.S. Copyright" (Ed.D. diss., University of Colorado, 1976).
6. Miller, "An Evaluation of Publishers' Responses," pp. 92-93.
7. Ibid.
8. Ibid.
9. *Audiovisual Market Place: A Multimedia Guide* (New York: Bowker, annual).
10. Jerome K. Miller, "WAECT Copyright Survey," *Resources for Teaching and Learning* 11, no. 1 (Fall 1974):16-17; "Consumer Disorientation," *EPIEGram; The Educational Consumers' Newsletter* 5, no. 3 (November 1, 1976):1-2.
11. The American Law Institute and the National Conference of Commissioners on Uniform State Laws, *Uniform Commercial Code, 1972 Official Text, with Comments and Appendix* (Philadelphia & Chicago: The Associations, 1972), sec. 2-207.

Chapter 5
Securing copyright protection

1. *United States Code,* Title 17, "Copyrights," sec. 101. Hereafter cited as Copyright Law.
2. Ibid., sec. 401(c).
3. Ibid., sec. 409.
4. Ibid., sec. 708(a)(1).
5. Ibid., sec. 408(b).
6. *Washingtonian* v. *Pearson,* 306 U.S. 30, 59 S.Ct. 397 (1939).
7. Copyright Law, sec. 407(d).
8. Ibid., sec. 402(c).
9. Ibid., sec. 101.
10. Ibid.
11. Ibid., sec. 201(c).
12. Ibid., sec. 403.
13. Ibid., sec. 406(c).
14. Ibid., sec. 401(b).
15. Ibid., sec. 406(b).
16. Ibid., sec. 405(a).
17. Ibid., sec. 405(b).
18. Ibid., sec. 405(c).

Index

Compiled by
Mary L. Mallory

Index